California

California

Ann Heinrichs

Children's Press®
A Division of Grolier Publishing
New York   London   Hong Kong   Sydney
Danbury, Connecticut

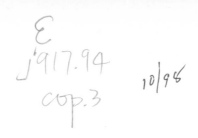

Frontispiece: Bixby Bridge

Front cover: The Golden Gate Bridge

Back cover: El Capitan and Bridal Falls, Yosemite National Park

Consultant: James J. Rawls, Ph.D., Diablo Valley College, California

Please note: All statistics are as up-to-date as possible at the time of publication.

Visit Children's Press on the Internet at http://publishing.grolier.com

Book production by Editorial Directions, Inc.

Library of Congress Cataloging-in-Publication Data

Heinrichs, Ann.
     California / by Ann Heinrichs.
        p. cm. — (America the beautiful. Second series)
     Includes bibliographical references (p.) and index.
     Summary : A brief introduction to the geography, history, natural resources,
industries, cities, and people of California.
     ISBN 0-516-20631-1
     California—Juvenile literature. [1. California.] I. Title. II. Series.
     861.3.H45 1998
     979.4—dc21   98-5225
                                                               CIP
                                                               AC

Acknowledgments

I am grateful to innumerable employees of California's trade and commerce agency, agriculture department, and state library for their kind assistance in this project; and to my sister, Jane Heinrichs Hsieh, for showing me the hidden delights of the Bay Area and the North Coast.

Mount Whitney

Point Sur

San Francisco cable car

Contents

California condor

Disneyland

Californians

La Brea Tar Pits

Giant panda

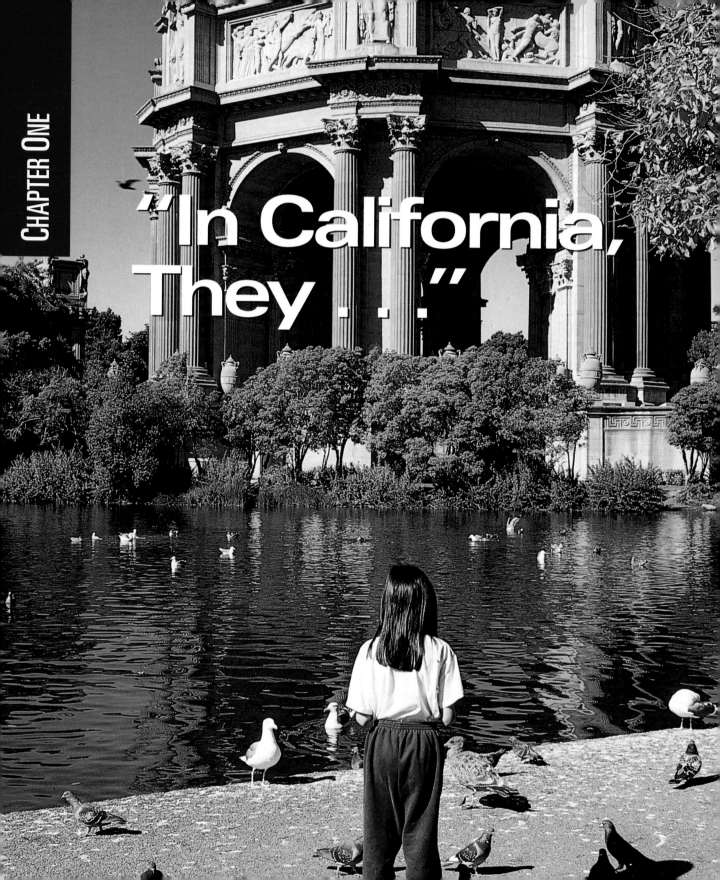

CHAPTER ONE

"In California, They . . ."

Rosa and Lieu are best friends. Both make straight *A*'s in junior-high English, and both want to be writers. But when they're at home with their families, Rosa speaks Spanish and Lieu speaks Vietnamese.

Rosa and Lieu are not unusual. More than a million California schoolchildren speak a language other than English at home. These languages include not only Spanish and Vietnamese, but also Hmong, Cantonese, Punjabi, and Russian, among others.

The school system is only a reflection of the state as a whole. California is the most ethnically diverse state in the nation. Almost half the state's population is made up of Latinos and people of Asian, African, and Native American ancestry. By the year 2001, these groups are expected to represent more than half the population.

Diversity is the one word that best describes California. The state is a tapestry of many colors, a crazy quilt of contrasts and extremes. The landscape ranges from snowy ski slopes to parched desert sands. Residents range from bodybuilders on sunny beaches

Children of all races attend school together in California.

Opposite: The Palace of Fine Arts, San Francisco

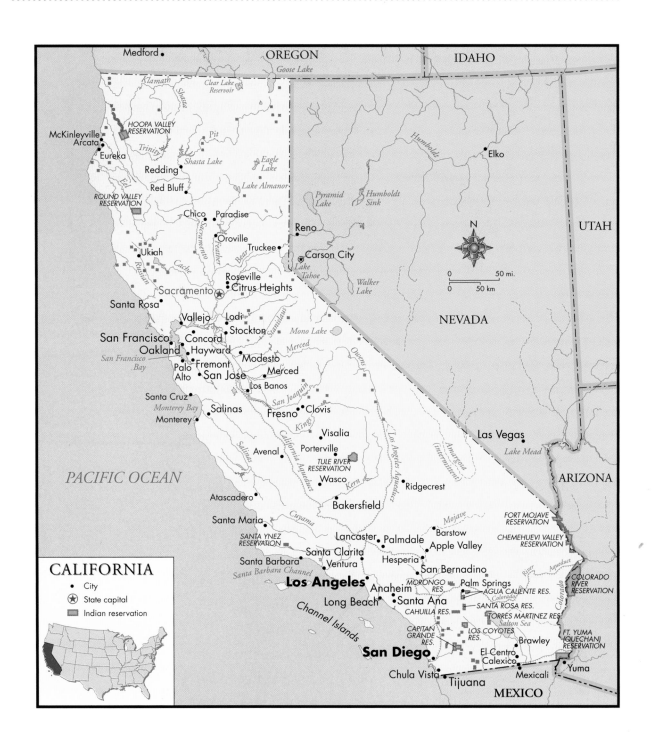

CALIFORNIA

- • City
- ⊛ State capital
- ▦ Indian reservation

to glitzy movie stars in limousines to middle-class suburbanites in ranch-style homes.

California also has an easygoing tolerance for different points of view. It embraces every imaginable type of religion, spiritual movement, philosophy, lifestyle, clothing style, and entertainment. As one tourist said, he'd believe any sentence that started with "In California, they . . .".

Accepting strangers and different customs has a long history in California. The Gold Rush that began in 1849 brought settlers from all parts of the globe. Protestant Swedes, Jewish New Yorkers, Catholic Chileans, and Taoist Chinese might all have rubbed shoulders in one day. People learned to keep their own traditions and let others keep theirs.

Besides offering personal freedom, California had a great climate, good jobs, and the richest farmland in the world. To millions looking for a better life, it was the Promised Land. As the movie, computer, and military industries blossomed, millions more headed west seeking their California dreams.

Today, about one out of every eight people in the United States is a Californian. "In California, they . . ." find a fantastic place to live, work, and play.

Opposite: Geopolitical map of California

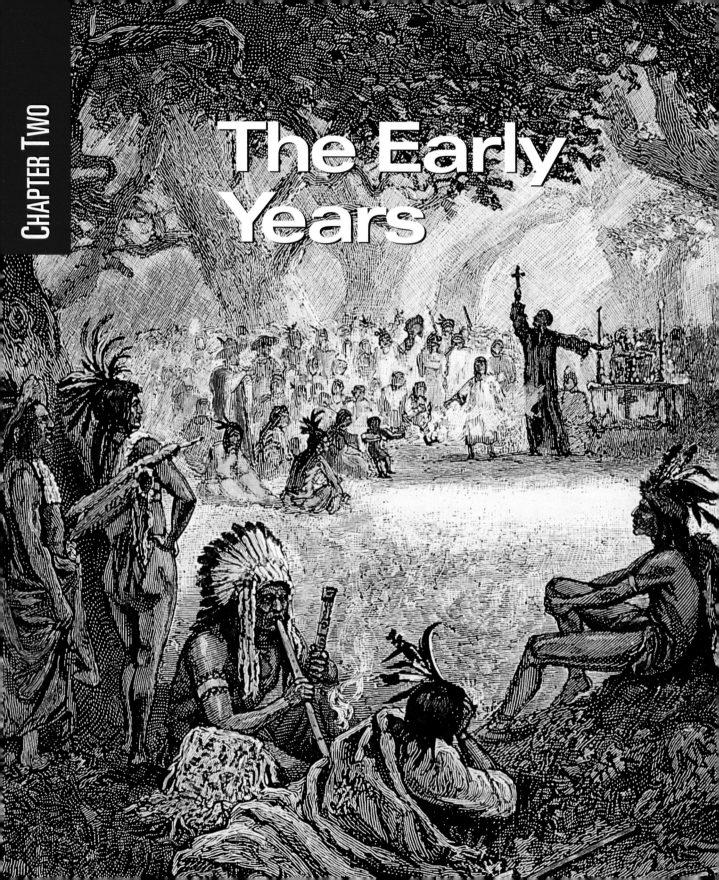

Chapter Two

The Early Years

Far across the ocean from Spain lay a fabulous island, a tropical paradise full of griffins and gold. It was California, the domain of Queen Calafía and her lost tribe of Amazons. Spaniards knew of this land from the romantic novel *The Adventures of Esplandián*, by Garci Rodríguez de Montalvo (1510).

When Spanish explorers came upon the peninsula of western Mexico, they were sure they had discovered that fantasy island. They named it California. Only later did they learn it was not an island at all but just a finger off the mainland to the north. So they called the narrow peninsula Baja California (Lower California) and the northern region Alta California (Upper California).

A life-size model of an Imperial mammoth stuck in La Brea Tar Pits

The First Californians

Of course, the Spaniards were latecomers to a land that others had discovered long before. Perhaps 15,000 years earlier, Asian people had crossed a land bridge from present-day Siberia to North America. That bridge is now submerged beneath Alaska's Bering Strait. The people spread south and east to inhabit what is now North and South America. Those in California were isolated by high mountains.

In far northwest California lived the Hupa people. The Maidu occupied central California, while the Quechan lived in the south.

Opposite: Jesuit missionaries in California

La Brea Tar Pits

About 35,000 years ago, where Los Angeles is now, oil began oozing up to the Earth's surface. Mixed with oxygen, it thickened into gummy black tar. Rainwater collected on top of the tar, and when animals came to drink, their feet got caught in the tar. There they stuck until they died.

Thousands of years later, the bodies were completely covered over with tar. Indians used the tar to waterproof their boats, and settlers used it on their roofs. In 1906, a geologist discovered the fossilized animal bones. It was the largest collection of Pleistocene-era animals ever found.

In Hancock Park, Los Angeles, life-size replicas of the prehistoric victims re-create the scene. Reconstructed skeletons from the tar pits are displayed at the George C. Page Museum of La Brea Discoveries. They include mastodons, mammoths, saber-toothed cats, and a human female. Even today, almost a century after the discovery, paleontologists are still finding, cleaning, and classifying fossils from the tar pits. ▪

Ohlone people lived in the San Francisco area, and to the north were the Pomo. Cahuilla people roamed the arid regions around the San Jacinto Mountains. Karok, Mojave, Yokut, Paiute, and Modoc were some of California's other natives.

A Paiute woman working with a woven winnowing tray

Native Ways of Life

California's Indians lived in clans, or groups of related families. Among the many groups, more than 100 different languages were spoken. The shaman of a tribe was both a spiritual leader and a doctor.

For food, they fished, hunted bear and

other wild game, and gathered herbs, roots, nuts, seeds, and berries. In regions where Western pines grew, they ate piñon nuts. Where there were oak trees, acorns were a staple food. Using a stone mortar, the Indians pounded them into meal and added water to make an acorn mush. Then they dropped hot stones into the mush until it was cooked.

People in northern and central California wove intricate baskets to carry and store food and valuables, sift acorn meal, serve food, hold water, and cook. Mothers carried their babies on their backs in woven cradle baskets. Caps and moccasins were also woven of plant fibers. People who lived near the coast used shells as money.

The Spanish Period

In 1521, Hernán Cortés conquered Mexico and named it New Spain. He traveled to Baja California in 1534 but did not venture into present-day California. Juan Rodríguez Cabrillo, a Portuguese explorer working for Spain, was the first European to sight what is now the state of California. He sailed into San Diego Bay in 1542. It was Cabrillo who first called this land by the name California.

In 1579, the English navigator Francis Drake cruised along the California coast. At

Spanish explorer
Hernán Cortés

Drake's Bay in present-day Marin County, he landed and met with Miwok Indians. According to Drake, they lived in earth-covered houses that were "very warme" and used woven reed bowls. Drake named this land "New Albion" before sailing on. ("Albion" was a poetic nickname for England.)

On a voyage in 1602, Sebastián Vizcaíno landed at several spots and gave them names. Some of these places were San Diego, San Clemente, Catalina Island, Santa Barbara, Carmel, and Monterey.

English navigator Francis Drake

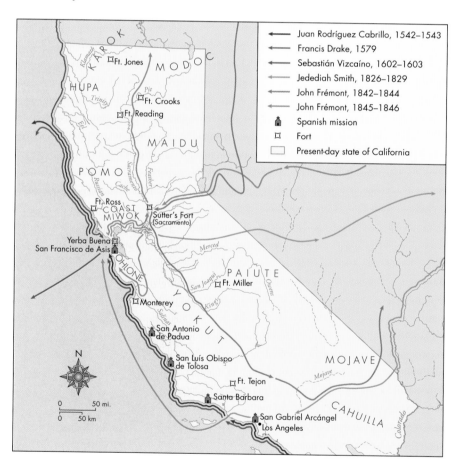

Exploration of California

Missions and Presidios

Gaspar de Portolá, the Spanish governor of Baja California, enlisted Franciscan friar Junípero Serra to build missions in the new territory. In 1769, Serra opened his first mission—San Diego de Alcalá in present-day San Diego. Near many of the missions, Portolá set up *presidios*, or military forts. San Diego's presidio opened in 1769 and Monterey's in 1770. A presidio and Mission Dolores marked the founding of San Francisco in 1776.

Father Junípero Serra

At Portolá's direction, other missionaries opened more missions up the coast. By 1823, a string of twenty-one missions stretched from San Diego up to Sonoma. Many were about a day's journey apart. The padres (fathers) taught the Indians Christianity, farming, and crafts. With Indian labor, they built churches and operated vast farms and ranches. Captivity, forced labor, and European diseases were a bitter pill for the Indians, though. Runaways and Indian uprisings were common.

In 1812, Russian fur traders set up Fort Ross on California's northwest coast. The Russian settlement made Spanish officials nervous. Nevertheless, it thrived on hunting sea otters for twenty years.

The Mexican Period

Mexico won its freedom from Spain in 1821, but the new nation practically ignored California. Mexican officials governed the territory, but the presidios were weak and ineffective. The Monterey presidio had three guns but hardly any gunpowder. San Francisco's presidio had ten rusty guns but no soldiers to fire them.

The new Mexican government disbanded California's mis-

John C. Frémont

Explorer John Charles Frémont (1813–1890) led the U.S. government's first overland expedition into California in the 1840s. He helped win California from Mexico in the Mexican War and served as one of California's first two U.S. senators (1850–1851). Frémont later became the nation's first Republican presidential candidate (1856) but lost to James Buchanan. ■

sions and gave the land to private farmers and ranchers. Many of these estates went to the *Californios*—Mexican merchants and soldiers. They turned their land grants into huge *ranchos*—a name used for farms as well as ranches.

Then began the great westward migration of settlers from the United States. Jedediah Smith was the first to arrive overland. He trudged across the Mojave Desert in 1826 and became the first white man to cross the Sierra Nevada mountain range. The first of many wagon trains to California left Missouri in 1841. Many travelers died in cholera epidemics or Indian attacks. The fate of the Donner party was especially tragic. Of the eighty-seven men, women, and children in the party, almost half starved or froze to death in the Sierra Nevada.

Most of the new settlers were just small-scale farmers or shopkeepers. But some began to be powerful merchants and government officials. Soon, not even the Californios expected that Mexico could hang on to California much longer. One "troublemaker" was John C. Frémont, a U.S. Army surveyor. He defied Mexican officials by raising the American flag near Monterey.

The Bear Flag Revolt

Texas was another territory that belonged to Mexico at this time. As in California, more and more American settlers had been moving in. Yankees in Texas finally fought Mexico and won their independence in 1836. That gave Californians the idea to take over their territory, too.

In June 1846, a handful of settlers in Sonoma stitched together a crude flag showing a bear and a star. Up went the flag as they

During the Bear Flag Revolt of 1846, a group of settlers seized the town of Sonoma, raised the Bear Flag, and proclaimed the California Republic.

declared the California Republic, with William B. Ide as president. This incident became known as the Bear Flag Revolt.

In July, a U.S. Navy fleet sailed into San Francisco Bay. Commodore John Sloat raised the American flag, declaring California a U.S. territory. The bold new California Republic had lasted only a month.

Meanwhile, Texas had become a U.S. state. In the dispute over its boundaries, the Mexican-American War broke out. It ended with a U.S. victory. On February 2, 1848, the two nations drew up the terms of their agreement in the Treaty of Guadalupe Hidalgo. Mexico ceded about half of its entire territory—including California—to the United States.

The treaty came just in time. Only nine days earlier, an obscure carpenter named James Wilson Marshall had changed the history of California forever.

CHAPTER THREE

Gold, Railroads, and the Promised Land

n January 24, 1848, James Marshall was hard at work on the south fork of the American River. He was building a sawmill for his boss, a Swiss immigrant named John Sutter. Marshall fingered an odd gray lump he'd picked from the water.

In 1848, James Marshall discovered gold while he was building a sawmill.

"Fool's gold," he thought. The glistening mineral pyrite had tricked many a miner, but not him. Just to be sure, Marshall pounded it with a stone. Pyrite was hard as a shovel blade, but this nugget squashed flat. It was gold! Marshall, as he wrote in his diary, "sat down and began to think right hard."

Of course, Marshall did more than think. He also talked. By the end of May, San Francisco was almost deserted, as so many men had left in search of gold.

The Gold Rush Is On!

"Picture us in a smoking kitchen, grinding coffee, toasting a herring, and peeling onions." That's how the mayor of Monterey described himself and the territorial governor. No one was left to do ordinary jobs—they'd all headed for the hills. Soldiers left their posts, and sailors jumped ship. They were now gold prospectors, swarming like ants over the hills around Sacramento.

By June, word had spread to the rest of the country. Could the gold rumors be true? In December, President James Polk himself assured Americans that it was. Suddenly, people who had never dreamed of leaving home decided to go for the gold. Thousands of

Opposite: Panning for gold during the California Gold Rush

ox-drawn wagons snaked west across the plains as "gold fever" ripped through the country.

Others came by boat. By February 1849, 130 ships had left the U.S. East Coast for California. A year later, the number was up to 17,000. Shiploads of gold hunters embarked from Mexico, South America, Hawaii, Australia, and even Europe. History remembers them all as the "Forty-Niners," named for the Gold Rush year of 1849.

The mining frenzy centered around Sacramento, the hub for the northern mines, and Stockton, the gateway to the southern mines. To reach either spot, a prospector started out from San Francisco. Most incoming ships landed in San Francisco, too.

San Francisco

San Francisco became a wild-and-woolly boomtown. Streets were muddy and unpaved. Deserted ships clogged the harbor, and canvas

Levi Strauss

In 1853, Levi Strauss (1829–1902) left New York City for San Francisco. He set up a dry-goods store to serve the burgeoning Gold Rush population. He was a successful merchant for twenty years; then in 1872, he got a letter from a tailor named Jacob Davis. Mr. Davis had invented a process to put metal rivets in men's denim pants to make them stronger for miners and other working men. Strauss and Davis received a patent for this process in 1873 and began to manufacture the first blue jeans in two factories in San Francisco. Now people all over the world wear Levi's jeans. The original factories were destroyed in the earthquake and fire of 1906, but a new factory was built and continues to operate. Levi's descendants still own the company: the chief executive officer of Levi Strauss & Company is the great-great-grandnephew of Levi himself. ■

tents carpeted the hills. Money flowed, and prices were high. One new arrival had to pay $1.50 to be rowed from his ship to the shore. A bushel of apples brought $125. One man bought a plot of land for $15 in 1847 and sold it for $40,000 after the gold discovery.

Lucky miners paid for food, drink, and lodging with gold nuggets or bags of gold dust. More gold changed hands in the dozens of gambling saloons that lined the streets. Entertainment was provided, but people could scarcely hear the honky-tonk piano over the raucous crowds.

Mining Camps

Mining camps were rough-and-ready colonies of tents, canvas shanties, and log cabins. Salt pork, biscuits, and molasses were the daily fare. Fresh meat and bread were rare treats. And no camp was complete without a gambling saloon, where knives and pistols settled the frequent brawls.

Every morning, the miners loaded up their pack mules with picks, shovels, and pans. Off they trudged to scour the hills and ra-

Working the gold mines

vines. They hoped to spy a band of gold in the rock or gold flecks in the silt dredged up from muddy riverbeds. Only the distant growling of a grizzly bear broke their single-minded toil.

When someone thought he'd struck a deposit of gold, he filed a claim. But it could be quite expensive to develop a mine till it paid off. A miner may have had to dig channels, redirect streams, and remove stones to get closer to the gold.

By the time the rush died down, the mines had yielded about $2 billion worth of gold. Most miners found nothing, though, and many went broke in the process. They laid their golden dreams aside and became farmers or merchants. Yet they remembered the old days with a popular song:

Though few and old, our hearts are bold
Yet oft do we repine
For the days of old, for the days of gold,
For the days of Forty-Nine.

Historical map of California

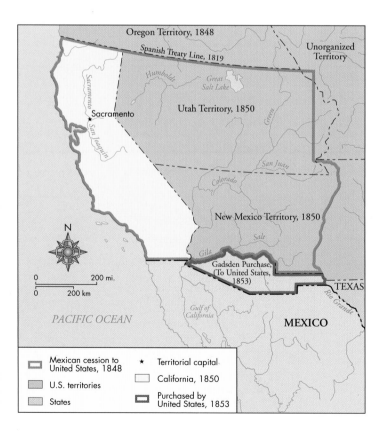

Statehood

After California was transferred to the United States in 1848, citizens were ready to set up their own government. But they heard nothing from Washington. Congress was busy trying to keep a balance between slave and nonslave states.

Impatient citizens held meetings about California's future. Some even wanted to make California a separate country. Thanks to the Gold Rush, the territory's population was exploding. It badly needed a government. Finally, in 1850, Congress approved statehood for California, making it the thirty-first state of the Union.

California Joins the Union

In September 1849, forty-eight delegates met in Monterey. They formed a legislature, drew up a constitution, and declared themselves the state of California. Voters ratified the constitution on November 13 and elected a governor.

Meanwhile, back in Washington, congressmen haggled over the question. In 1850, they voted their approval. President Millard Fillmore signed the California statehood bill on September 9, 1850. San Franciscans celebrated Statehood Day on October 29 with a great procession in the city plaza (above). ■

The Railroads Arrive

"Those tourist cars weren't very pleasant traveling, but they were a lot better than six months of oxen and wagon. We had to furnish our own bedding, even the mattresses, which were made of ticking filled with straw, so they could be thrown away at the end. We had to furnish our own food, too. There was a stove in the corner of one end, where we women cooked. I have forgotten just how many were in the car, but I do remember there were sixteen children, so you can imagine the hubbub. . . . We had our own brooms, with which we had to sweep the car, too."

—Mrs. Hortense Watkins,
who took her four children west by train

In the 1860s, many Chinese laborers helped to build the railroads.

In the 1860s, railroad owners shipped in thousands of Chinese laborers to help build the transcontinental railroad. Chinese people made up 80 percent of the labor force that laid tracks for the western portion of the route. By 1869, tracks stretched across the nation, all the way to Sacramento. Now people and goods could ride the rails from coast to coast.

Like the Watkins clan, whole families rode the rails to California. Children traveled for half fare. The trip from Kansas to California took ten days, but, as Hortense Watkins said, it beat a six-month wagon ride. By 1870, more than half a million people lived in California.

The San Francisco Earthquake

"I was suddenly awakened soon after 5 o'clock . . . to a realization of being shaken by an earthquake that seemed to threaten to tear our house to pieces. The building danced a lively jig, jumping up and down a good part of a foot at every jump, at the same time swaying this way and that; the walls and ceilings were twisting and squirming, as if wrestling to tear themselves asunder. . . . Then there were the terrifying noises, the cracking and creaking of timber, the smashing and crashing of falling glass, bric-a-brac, and furniture, and the thumping of falling bricks coursing down the roof sides from the chimney tops. . . . I lay in bed and saw the debris of wrecked chimney tops go sailing down past our bedroom windows."

—Newspaperman Frank Leach

The devastation of the 1906 San Francisco earthquake

This was the scene in San Francisco on the early morning of April 18, 1906. Worse than the quake itself was the fire. The tremor broke gas pipelines and knocked over stoves, lanterns, and candles. In no time, the city was ablaze as wooden buildings went up in flames. Water pipes had burst, too, so firefighters didn't have the water pressure they needed to put out the fire.

"It was a terrible sight," Leach wrote. "Flames were leaping high in the air. . . . Great clouds of black smoke filled the sky and hid the rays of the sun." The fires raged for three days, destroying most of the downtown area and many neighborhoods. As many as 3,000 people lost their lives, and 225,000—more than half the population—were left homeless. San Franciscans rebuilt their city within a few years, though.

The Early Twentieth Century

David Horsley, a New York film producer, decided to shoot his movie *The Law of the Range* in Hollywood. That was in 1911. Within a year, several big movie companies moved from New York to Hollywood. The sunny climate and natural scenery made it a perfect location for filmmaking.

All of a sudden, Hollywood was the moviemaking capital of the world. In big cities and small towns alike, movie buffs lined up to see their favorite Hollywood stars. Some of the earliest were Rudolph Valentino, Charlie Chaplin, Clara Bow, Mary Pickford, Douglas Fairbanks, and cowboy actor William Hart.

Californians were thrilled when the Panama Canal opened in 1914. The new canal provided a sea route between the Atlantic and Pacific oceans through Central America. Before that, a ship from the

U.S. East Coast had to sail all the way around the tip of South America to get to California.

To celebrate the opening of the canal—and to show itself off—California held two grand exhibitions in 1915: the Panama-Pacific International Exposition in San Francisco and the Panama-California Exposition in San Diego.

Manufacturing and heavy industry grew during World War I (1914–1918) as battleships, rubber tires, and other wartime equipment rolled off California's assembly lines. After the war, California embarked on public water projects. Dams, canals, and aqueducts brought irrigation into the Central Valley and water supplies into the cities.

Douglas Fairbanks and Mary Pickford were among Hollywood's first movie stars.

Cecil B. deMille

Cecil Blount deMille (1881–1959), pioneer film producer and director, helped make Hollywood the movie capital of the world. Born into a theater family, he first tried his hand at acting and scriptwriting. In 1912, he helped start a movie studio that became Paramount Pictures.

DeMille's first feature-length Hollywood movie, *The Squaw Man*, opened in 1913. He was the first director to use a megaphone and loudspeakers to give orders on the set. He made seventy films in his career. His best-known works are multimillion-dollar epics such as *The Ten Commandments* (1923 and 1956), *The King of Kings* (1926), *Samson and Delilah* (1949), and *The Greatest Show on Earth* (1952). ∎

The Great Depression

In 1929, the nation plunged into the horrors of the Great Depression. Banks and businesses failed, and swarms of jobless people were out on the streets. Some sold apples; others just begged. On top of that, drought and erosion turned the Great Plains into a Dust Bowl in the mid-1930s. Farmers gazed in despair at their parched and barren fields.

To millions who were down and out, California was the Promised Land. Just as covered wagons lumbered across the plains in the Gold Rush, now caravans of rickety cars and trucks snaked westward, piled high with kitchen tables, bulging trunks, and beds. John Steinbeck's novel *The Grapes of Wrath* tells the sorry tale of the Joads, a migrant family from Oklahoma.

So many homeless, jobless people poured into California that the state passed a law to keep them out. But the U.S. Supreme Court declared the law unconstitutional, so the flood of people kept coming. Between 1920 and 1940, California's population more than doubled, from 3.4 million to 6.9 million people.

Opposite: Many families, such as this one, moved to California to escape the drought of the Great Plains in the 1930s.

CHAPTER FOUR

Modern Times

World War II (1939–1945) transformed California into a modern, industrial state. In December 1941, after Japan bombed the U.S. naval base at Pearl Harbor, Hawaii, the United States entered the war. Soon airplanes, ships, and weapons were rolling off the assembly lines in California's factories. California became the top state in the nation for aircraft production.

The Manzanar Japanese internment camp

During the war, Japanese Americans became targets of fear and suspicion. Newspapers and politicians warned that they could be dangerous to national security. The U.S. government had more than 100,000 Japanese Americans (the majority of them Californians) in camps until the war was over. In California, Manzanar was the main Japanese prison camp.

In fact, there were no instances of Japanese-American spying or sabotage. More than 20,000 men and women of Japanese ancestry served in the U.S. Army during the war. In 1988, the U.S. paid reparations to those who had been imprisoned.

In 1945, as the war drew to a close, California was the scene of a major event in world history. Delegates from fifty nations met in San Francisco and founded the United Nations.

Opposite: Paramount Pictures, Los Angeles, 1947

The gang from *The Mickey Mouse Club* of the 1950s

The Fifties

After the war, new suburbs sprang up, and new freeways connected them. Streets were lined with easily built, one-story ranch-style homes. Around the country, the ranch style became the fashion for mass housing. New kitchens glistened with labor-saving appliances.

The television set, a new invention, soon became the entertainment center in the home. California's movie industry quickly expanded to include TV studios. Across the country, kids learned about life from California-based TV shows such as *The Mickey Mouse Club* and *I Love Lucy*.

In the 1950s, the United States and the Soviet Union were engaged in a political rivalry called the cold war. For California, this meant more business for the state's defense industries. Communism, the Soviet Union's political system, was seen as an ever-present danger. One prominent anti-Communist in the U.S. Congress was Richard Nixon, California's own congressman. During the cold war era, many members of Hollywood's movie community were suspected of being Communists. Some were blacklisted, or labeled as undesirable. Dozens of actors traveled to Washington, D.C., to show support for their co-workers.

The Sixties and Beyond

American society was changing in the 1960s, and Californians led the way. Pop music and Hollywood beach movies saturated the nation with California's beach culture. Surfers and bikini-clad girls became teenagers' ideals. But soon, more serious issues arose.

In 1964, students at the University of California at Berkeley led the free speech movement. They demanded the right to promote their political opinions on campus—an activity the school banned at that time. More student demonstrations targeted the Vietnam War, nuclear weapons, and racial inequality. Across the nation, campus riots led to violence and school shutdowns.

The summer of 1967 was called the "summer of love." "Make love, not war" was the motto for 100,000 flower-bedecked hippies gathered in San Francisco's Haight-Ashbury district. To the sounds of rock music, they celebrated the dawning of a new age of peace and love, while police tried to control the crowds.

Richard Nixon

Richard Milhous Nixon (1913–1994), born in Yorba Linda, was the only native Californian to be elected president. As a U.S. congressman (1947–1951), his anti-Communist views on the House Un-American Activities Committee drew attention. Nixon served as a U.S. senator (1951–1953) and as vice-president (1953–1961) under Dwight D. Eisenhower. Nixon was elected thirty-seventh U.S. president in 1968 and re-elected in 1972. In 1974, in connection with the Watergate scandal, he became the first U.S. president to resign.

Highlights of Nixon's presidency included opening trade relations with the People's Republic of China and ending the Vietnam War. ■

Ronald Reagan

Ronald Wilson Reagan (1911–) born in Tampico, Illinois, was the fortieth president of the United States. As an actor, he appeared in more than fifty movies and served as president of the Screen Actors Guild. As governor of California (1967–1975), he worked to lower state taxes and reform the welfare system. Reagan, a conservative Republican, served two terms as president (1981–1989). His economic policies lowered taxes and government spending but raised the federal debt. In foreign affairs, he fought terrorists in the Middle East and aided anti-Communist guerrillas in Nicaragua. ■

Conservative values lived side by side with these liberal movements. Ronald Reagan, a conservative Republican, was California's governor from 1967 to 1975.

In 1978, California voters approved Proposition 13. It drastically lowered property taxes but also took funds away from public schools.

Californians watched several of their own leaders rise to national prominence. Earl Warren, a former governor of California, was chief justice of the U.S. Supreme Court from 1953 to 1969. Two California Republicans became president of the United States: Richard Nixon (1969–1974) and Ronald Reagan (1981–1989).

Today's Issues

Today, California faces many of the same issues that trouble the rest of the nation. As in other American cities, California's urban areas deal with gangs, drugs, and violence. In the mid-1990s, California had the nation's third-highest rate of violent crime. Race relations are often tense. In 1992, south-central Los Angeles erupted in riots when white police officers were acquitted of brutality toward an African-American man.

California voters are waging fierce battles over ethnic issues. In 1994, they passed a measure to cut back on affirmative action for minorities in state agencies and schools. Other ballot measures targeted welfare benefits for illegal immigrants and bilingual education in the public schools.

The environment and public health are hot issues, too. Loggers have violent run-ins with activists who want to save endangered redwood trees and Northern spotted owls. Industrial pollution contaminates rivers and lakes. To combat air pollution, California passed stiff regulations for vehicle emissions in the 1960s. In 1998, it became the first state in the nation to ban smoking in bars.

Firefighters battling a blaze after two days of rioting in Los Angeles, 1992

Since the 1970s, the stampede of new residents into California has slowed down. Cuts in defense spending have put thousands out of work. An economic recession in the 1990s hurt many other businesses. In addition, earthquakes in San Francisco and Los Angeles—plus devastating wildfires and mudslides—are making some people wonder if California is a safe place to live.

But it's still the fastest-growing state in the nation. In the twenty-first century, as in times past, millions more are sure to embrace California as the Promised Land.

CHAPTER FIVE

California Landscapes

California sits at the meeting place of two tectonic plates, shifting sections of the Earth's crust. The Pacific Plate holds most of the Pacific Ocean floor, plus California's present-day coast. The North American Plate carries most of the North American continent.

Like all sections of the Earth's crust, these plates have been on the move for millions of years. About 150 million years ago, they started smashing together. Instead of crashing head-on, the Pacific Plate slipped under the edge of North America. From underneath, it pushed up the Sierra Nevada mountains.

The same uplifting motion formed the much younger Cascade range of northern California, Oregon, and Washington State. Here, the pressure between the plates generated heat so intense that it melted the rocky crust. Volcanoes erupted, spewing out ash and molten rock.

The Cascade Mountains

Opposite: Junipers and pines in the Sierra Nevada

John Muir

Explorer and naturalist John Muir (1838–1914) was born in Scotland and moved to the United States at age eleven. He arrived in California in 1868 and began studying the Yosemite Valley. An ardent champion of forest conservation, he helped establish Yosemite and Sequoia National Parks. Muir founded the Sierra Club and persuaded President Theodore Roosevelt to reserve millions of acres of U.S. forestland as national forests. Muir Woods National Monument, near San Francisco, is one of many California sites named after him. ■

Pacific islands lying offshore were crushed against the shoreline. In the force of the collision, the land buckled and warped to form California's coastal ranges. That left a long valley between the coastal mountains and the Sierra Nevada.

After the collision, as the plates kept shifting, southeastern California stretched and sank. The result was Death Valley, the lowest spot on the North American continent.

The San Andreas Fault is the place where the two shifting plates meet. The North American Plate is still drifting westward, while the Pacific Plate pushes east and north. Their movement is so slow that, we don't notice it. But as the plates keep grinding against

Notable California Earthquakes

Year	Richter Magnitude*	Location
1769	6.0	Los Angeles Basin
1857	8.3	Fort Tejon
1865	6.5	Santa Cruz Mountains
1868	7.0	Hayward Fault
1872	7.6	Owens Valley
1906	8.3	San Francisco
1922	7.3	West of Eureka
1923	7.2	Cape Mendocino
1933	6.3	Long Beach
1940	7.1	Imperial Valley
1952	7.7	Kern County
1971	6.6	San Fernando Valley
1983	6.7	Coalinga
1989	7.1	Loma Prieta (San Francisco area)
1992	7.4	Landers/Big Bear
1994	6.7	Northridge (San Fernando Valley)

*Richter magnitudes before the 1940s are estimated, based on effects.

each other, the friction causes devastating earthquakes along the fault.

Boundaries

California is the nation's third-largest state, after Alaska and Texas. On the west, the Pacific Ocean carves out 1,264 miles (2,034 km) of beaches and bays. On the southeast, the Colorado River marks the jagged border with Arizona.

California's western border is the Pacific Ocean, seen here at Point Sur.

California's other borders were drawn in straight lines. The northern border cuts right through the Klamath and Cascade mountains, with Oregon on the other side. On the east, two long lines carve out a border with Nevada. A short line on the south marks California's international border with Mexico.

Mountains Ever in Sight

"Go where you may within the bounds of California, mountains are ever in sight."

—John Muir in *The Mountains of California* (1894)

The Sierra Nevada is the highest mountain range in North America. Its granite peaks are still growing. Mount Whitney, in the southern or High Sierra, is the highest point in the continental United States. The western face of the Sierra is a gradual rise, with wooded slopes. But the eastern face is steep and, in some places, a sheer drop. For mountain climbers, it's a formidable challenge.

Lake Tahoe, in the Sierra Nevada, is the largest and deepest alpine lake in North America. There's enough water in Lake Tahoe to cover all of California with 14 inches (36 cm) of water.

Many mountains in the Cascade range are still considered active volcanoes. They're part of the Ring of Fire, the great circle of volcano-ridden coastland around the Pacific Ocean. Other volcanoes in the Ring of Fire are Washington State's Mount St. Helens and Indonesia's Krakatoa.

Mount Shasta is the second-highest peak in the Cascade range, after Washington State's Mount Rainier. Lassen Peak, also in the Cascades, hasn't erupted since 1921. But molten rock deep below the region keeps mudpots and sulfur pools steaming and boiling on the Modoc Plateau.

In northwest California are

California's Geographical Features

Total area; rank	158,648 sq. mi. (410,896 sq km); 3rd
Land; rank	155,973 sq. mi. (403, 968 sq km); 3rd
Water; rank	2,896 sq. mi. (7,501 sq km); 12th
Inland water; rank	2,674 sq. mi. (6,926 sq km); 8th
Coastal water; rank	222 sq. mi. (575 sq km); 16th
Geographic center	38 miles (61 km) east of Madera
Highest point	Mount Whitney, 14,494 feet (4,418 m)
Lowest point	Death Valley, 282 feet (86 m) below sea level
Largest city	Los Angeles
Longest river	Sacramento River, 382 miles (615 km)
Population; rank	29,839,250 (1990 census); 1st
Record high temperature	134°F (57°C) at Greenland Ranch in Death Valley on July 10, 1913
Record low temperature	−45°F (−43°C), at Boca, near Truckee, on January 20, 1937
Average July temperature	75°F (24°C)
Average January temperature	44°F (7°C)
Annual precipitation	22 inches (56 cm)

the steep slopes and deep canyons of the Klamath Mountains. To the south, the coast ranges line the shore all the way to Santa Barbara County. The only natural break in this range is San Francisco Bay.

Around Santa Barbara, the coast mountains continue as the Transverse and Peninsular Mountains. These ranges run east-west rather than north-south. The Transverse ranges, surrounding the Los Angeles area, include the Santa Ynez, Santa Monica, San Gabriel, and San Bernardino Mountains. The Peninsular ranges cover the San Diego County area and continue into Mexico.

Rivers and Valleys

California's major river systems are the Sacramento and San Joaquin rivers. They meet and form a delta as they empty into San

Opposite: Mount Whitney is the highest point in the continental United States.

San Francisco Bay

Francisco Bay. Clustered around the bay are dozens of communities that grew up because of the Gold Rush or farming or both. The largest of these are San Francisco, San Jose, Oakland, and Berkeley.

The Sacramento River and its tributaries drain northern California. Sacramento, the state capital, sits at the juncture of the Sacramento and American rivers. This is the northern mine region, where California's gold was discovered. The San Joaquin River system runs through central California. Stockton, an important river port during the Gold Rush, was known as the gateway to the southern mines.

The Sacramento and San Joaquin river basins form the long sweep of California's Central Valley. This is one of the most fertile farm regions in the world. Its rich soil is made of sediment that's been washing down from the mountains for hundreds of thousands of years. Besides Sacramento and Stockton, major cities in the valley are Fresno and Bakersfield.

In the far southeast, the Colorado River system is the major water source. Aqueducts and canals carry irrigation water from the river to the fields of the Imperial and Coachella Valleys.

In 1906, the Colorado River burst its banks, flooding the Imperial Valley. The water gathered to form the Salton Sea, and it never dried up again. Rainwater in the Imperial Valley flowed into it, as well as runoff from irrigated fields. Every year, it gets 4 million tons of salts from the soil. Now the Salton Sea is 25 percent saltier than the Pacific Ocean.

Deserts

South and east of the Sierra is the Great Basin that extends into Nevada, Utah, and Arizona. Much of this desolate wasteland is the Mojave Desert. Once the floor of an inland sea, the Mojave is now a high-elevation desert. Edwards Air Force Base is in the Mojave, as are the military bases of China Lake, Fort Irwin, and Twentynine Palms.

At the north edge of the Mojave is Death Valley. Badwater, in Death Valley, is 282 feet (86 m) below sea level. It's the lowest point in the state and in all of North America. It's only about 80 miles

California's topography

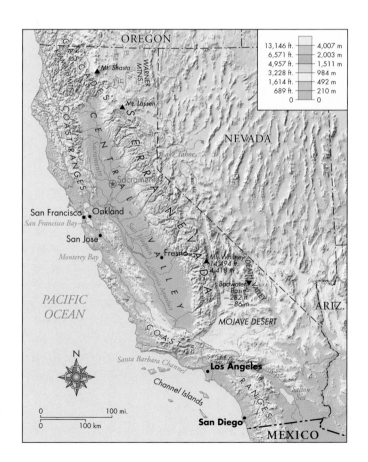

(129 km) from Mount Whitney, California's highest point.

The Colorado Desert covers far southeastern California. Here and there, underground springs create jewel-like oases of water and greenery. Resort towns such as Palm Springs have grown up at these sites.

Animals

Beavers, wildcats, muskrats, deer, black bears, mountain lions, and foxes roam the forests of California. Desert animals include coyotes, long-eared jackrabbits, tortoises, lizards, and rattlesnakes.

California's last grizzly bear was shot in 1922. The smaller black bears still live in the Sierra Nevada. Wolves have disappeared from the state, although plenty of coyotes remain. Pronghorn antelopes and Roosevelt elks, once nearly extinct, have now bounced back. The endangered San

Joaquin kit fox once roamed over much of central California. Now farms and cities, predator attacks, and hunting have made the kit fox an endangered species.

Jays, doves, owls, quail, and grouse are common in the forests. Waterbirds include ducks, geese, herons, seagulls, and pelicans. Cormorants, seen up and down the coast, strut about on Point Lobos in a great colony. Cactus wrens are a familiar species in the Mojave Desert. Bald and golden eagles, once plentiful, are now endangered.

The California condor is the largest land bird in North America, with a wingspan of

The California condor is the largest land bird in North America.

9 feet (2.7 m). Sadly, only a few still exist in the wild. They liked to nest in the giant sequoias, which are also disappearing fast. The San Diego Zoo is breeding condors to release back into the wild. Another endangered bird is the Nortern spotted owl.

California's rivers are home to striped bass, salmon, sturgeon, black bass, bluegill, catfish, and trout. Salmon and steelhead can be seen migrating up the Sacramento River to spawn every autumn. Offshore in the Pacific are rockfish, halibut, salmon, and shellfish such as abalone, clam, crab, shrimp, lobster, and scallops.

In the spring and fall, whale watchers gather along the coast to watch gray whales migrating. Sea lions, another marine mammal, get lots of attention, too. They like to lounge around Fisherman's Wharf in San Francisco, barking their heads off.

Opposite: The lowest point in North America is near Badwater in Death Valley.

The sea lions that gather at San Francisco's Fisherman's Wharf bark for the attention of many tourists.

Plants

The Mojave Desert is dotted with creosote, ocotillo, mesquite, cactus, and sage. The creosote bush is a shrub whose poisonous roots kill off any nearby vegetation. Barrel, cholla, and prickly pear are some of the many cactus varieties. They soak up water during rare rainfalls and store it for months, or even years. In Death Valley, almost the only plants that survive are hardy mesquite and creosote.

Mountains, valleys, and high deserts explode with color in the springtime. Golden poppies, coreopsis, heliotropes, evening primroses, lupine, and fireweed are among California's spectacular wildflowers. The ice plant, which covers coastal hillsides, bears beautiful flowers but is considered a pest.

The Joshua trees of the southern desert are not really trees but members of the yucca family. Religious-minded settlers believed their branches looked like the outstretched arms of the biblical figure Joshua.

Forests cover about two-fifths of the state. Mountains and hills are heavily forested, and much of this land is protected as national forests. Most of these areas consist of evergreens—pines, firs, cedars, junipers, and cypresses. Monterey pines are found around Monterey, and Torrey pines grow in San Diego County.

Stately palm trees line the boulevards in Los Angeles and other southern cities. Fan palms grow in the south, too, especially where they can reach underground water. Eucalyptus trees, imported from Australia in the 1800s, thrive in California's climate. Oaks are the most common deciduous trees (trees that shed their leaves every year). Willows and poplars are widespread, too.

The Tallest, Biggest, and Oldest

Two types of sequoia live in California: giant sequoias and coast redwoods. The redwoods that grow along the north and central coasts are the tallest trees in the world. In fact, the world's tallest tree is a coast redwood in the Tall Trees Grove of Redwood National Park. It stands 368 feet (112 m) tall.

In actual volume of wood, giant sequoias are the world's biggest trees. Giant sequoias once grew across most of North America, but the only specimens left in the world today grow in the High Sierra.

California's parks and forests

A giant sequoia named the General Sherman Tree is the world's biggest tree. The 2,500-year-old giant is 275 feet (84 m) high, and its trunk measures 103 feet (31 m) around.

Sequoias survive forest fires well because their bark is fire-resistant and very thick—as much as 18 inches (46 cm). Strangely enough, sequoias need fire to reproduce—it takes intense heat to make its seeds burst out of their casings. Every year, forest rangers set controlled fires to burn parts of the sequoia groves.

The General Sherman Tree

The General Sherman Tree is the biggest living thing in the world. It stands 275 feet (84 m) high—about the height of a 26-story building. Its trunk measures 103 feet (31 m) around. Coast redwoods are taller. They average 300–350 feet (91–107 m). But General Sherman wins with the greatest volume of wood—52,500 cubic feet (1,487 cu m). Nobody knows for sure how old General Sherman and the other giants are. But scientists guess they are between 1,800 and 2,700 years old. ■

The ancient bristlecone pine trees that grow in Inyo National Forest on the east slopes of the Sierra are the oldest living things in the world. Some are more than 4,700 years old. When Egypt's first pharaoh began his reign, they had already been alive for more than 1,500 years!

Climate and Weather

Along the coast, Californians enjoy warm, dry summers and mild winters. Summers are hotter in the Central Valley than on the coast. Desert winds sometimes blow across the Santa Ana Mountains into Los Angeles. Called the Santa Ana winds, they bring oppressive heat waves as hot as the desert. San Francisco is a

A view of pines and aspens in Inyo National Forest

foggy city. When the warm, wet ocean breezes hit the cool coastal current, the air condenses into fog.

For most of the state, the rainy season lasts from about November through April. Mountains in the northwest get heavy rainfall, while the deserts get almost none. The rains can be uneven, though. Droughts have led to devastating wildfires. At other times, heavy rains cause flash floods and mudslides that wash away hillside homes.

Sierra Nevada is Spanish for "snowy range." Heavy snows fall in the High Sierra just a short distance from the scorching desert sands. Good, reliable snowfall makes the Sierra Nevada a popular ski location. Squaw Valley was the site of the 1960 Winter Olympic Games. Melting snow also provides water for much of central and southern California.

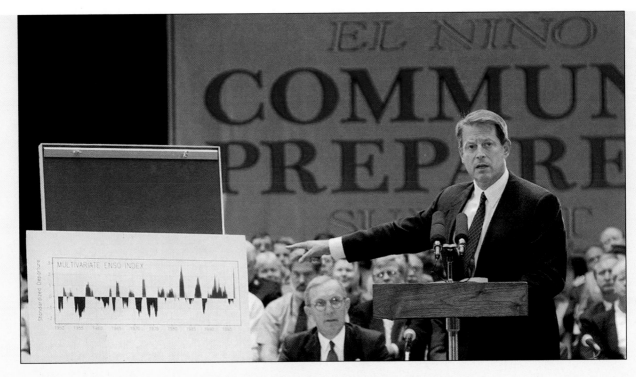

El Niño—The Troublesome Child

Californians have learned to watch out for "El Niño years." El Niño gets blamed for everything from torrential rains and floods to droughts and fires. Spanish for "The Child," El Niño is named after the baby Jesus. It got the name from its Christmastime appearance along the Pacific coast of South America.

El Niño is a warming of the upper layers of the Pacific Ocean. As the warm water evaporates, it forms heavy clouds that dump rain on coastal land.

Trade winds, blowing east to west, usually keep the warm waters in the western Pacific. But every two to seven years, the warm water breaks loose and heads for the South American coast. It first appears off the coast of Peru, then moves up to California. That's an El Niño year. Then the Americas get rain, while Asia's coast gets drought.

In reality, El Niño is just one of many climatic factors that work together to produce a weather event. Another impor-

tant factor is the California current. This is a cold ocean current that sweeps down the coast from Alaska.

While El Niño is not to blame for every weather disaster, scientists study it carefully. A nationwide El Niño summit meeting was held in October 1997 in Santa Monica (above). Meteorologists and politicians met there to discuss what El Niño might do in the coming years and how people can prepare for its effects. ■

CHAPTER SIX

California, from Top to Bottom

Lassen Peak, one of California's active volcanoes

Northeastern California is an unspoiled wilderness of river rapids, thick forests, snowcapped peaks, volcanoes, glaciers, and canyons. This area is called Shasta Cascade for Mount Shasta and its setting in the Cascade Range.

For Native Americans, the abode of the Sky Spirit was the snowy peak of Mount Shasta. This dormant volcano is the headwater of the Sacramento River. Downstream, the river becomes the thunderous waters of Shasta Dam. This 602-foot (183-m) dam, three times higher than Niagara Falls, has the highest spillway in the world.

Volcanoes created weird landscapes in the far northeast. In Lava Beds National Monument, molten rock once spewed and flowed for miles. It created a black and jagged landscape of lava beds, craters, and cinder cones. A network of lava-tube caves runs through the region. The caves were formed when the outer surface

Opposite: Mission San Diego de Alcalá

of a lava flow cooled and hardened, while the lava underneath kept flowing.

Lassen Volcanic National Park surrounds Lassen Peak, an active volcano. Its snowcapped crest makes it seem harmless, but boiling lakes and mudpots nearby are reminders that the Earth is churning not far below.

The North Coast and Wine Country

Majestic redwood forests line California's north coast, and powerful waves crash on the battered shores. South of Crescent City is Redwood National Park. Herds of Roosevelt elk roam through this preserve of coastal redwoods. Farther down the coast, visitors drive along the Avenue of the Giants. This scenic highway winds through breathtaking thickets of giant trees.

In Mendocino, Sonoma, and Napa counties, the climate is perfect for growing grapes. Highway 29 runs through Napa Valley, passing dozens of vineyards on rich, fertile soil. Many of the wineries offer tours and wine tastings.

Calistoga, at the valley's north end, is famous for its hot mineral springs and mud baths. Calistoga's "Old Faithful" geyser shoots water up about every forty minutes. In the nearby Petrified Forest lie redwood trees turned to stone millions of years ago after a volcanic eruption.

Sonoma County is steeped in history. Its mission, San Francisco Solano de Sonoma, was built there in 1823. Petaluma was the 1840 rancho of Mexican general Mariano Vallejo. In 1812, Russian seal hunters founded Fort Ross, now a state historic park. Writer Jack London's ranch in Glen Ellen is also a state historic park.

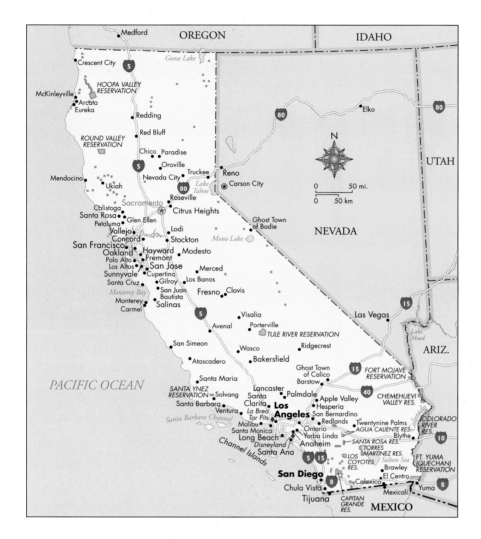

California's cities and interstates

Gold Country

Sacramento sits at the meeting point of the Sacramento and American rivers. It was once Johann Sutter's mill, but miners and tradesmen overran it. Sacramento was the end of the line for intrepid Pony Express riders. Eventually, it became the capital of the whole state.

The gold-domed state capitol in Sacramento

The capitol, completed in 1874, is one of the most beautiful buildings in California. High above the central lobby is an ornate cupola, or dome, topped by a gold-plated copper sphere. Several offices in the capitol are preserved as they looked 100 years ago. Visitors are welcome to watch the state legislature when it's in session.

Another historic building is the fifteen-room Governor's Mansion. Thirteen California governors lived in it from 1903 through 1967 before it became a museum.

Along the cobblestone streets of Old Sacramento historic district is the California State Railroad Museum. It displays a century of restored railroad cars, as well as model trains. On the waterfront is the *Delta King*, one of the luxurious paddleboats of the Sacramento River.

Coloma, east of Sacramento, is where James Marshall first discovered gold. Now it's a state historic site where people can pan for gold on the American River. To the north is Nevada City, where wealthy San Franciscans used to have their vacation homes.

East of Stockton is Calaveras County. Black Bart (Charles Bolton), called the "gentleman bandit," was once jailed in the county courthouse, now a museum. But the most famous spot in the county is Angels Camp. That's where Mark Twain latched onto the story of the jumping frog for "The Celebrated Jumping Frog of Calaveras County."

The Sierra Nevada

The high peaks of the Sierra Nevada tower over pine forests, meadows, and alpine lakes. Interstate 80 crosses the mountains

Yosemite National Park

Yosemite National Park covers almost 1,200 square miles (3,108 sq km) of scenic wilderness. It was set aside in 1890 to preserve part of the Sierra Nevada. Three groves of giant sequoias dominate the park. Unfortunately, Yosemite's famous drive-through tree—Wawona Tunnel Tree in the Mariposa Grove—fell in the winter of 1968–1969. ■

A view of Lake Tahoe from its eastern shore

through Donner Pass, where more than forty members of the Donner party perished in the cruel winter of 1846–1847. A 22-foot (6.7-m) monument to them matches the depth of the snow that winter.

The Sierra region encompasses Yosemite, and Sequoia and Kings Canyon National Parks. Yosemite, carved out by glaciers, became the nation's first national park in 1890. Sequoia and Kings Canyon adjoin each other, forming one continuous national park. Together, they cover about 1,300 square miles (3,367 sq km) of unspoiled forested peaks and canyons.

East of the Sierra is Bodie, a wild mining camp turned ghost town. To the south is Mono Lake, an ancient inland sea. Strange,

Sequoia and Kings Canyon National Parks

Sequoia and Kings Canyon National Parks join together as one continuous parkland. Sequoia (above) is the nation's second-oldest national park. One of the biggest attractions is the Giant Forest, containing four of the five largest sequoias in the world. The most famous is the General Sherman Tree, the largest living thing on Earth. Also in Sequoia is Mount Whitney, the highest peak in the continental United States.

Kings Canyon began as General Grant National Park. It's the home of the General Grant Tree, the third-largest tree in the world. Big Stump Basin contains giant sequoia stumps left from lumbering operations in the 1800s. The largest of all the sequoia groves is Redwood Canyon. ■

towering rock formations called tufa stick up out of the lake. Once deep underwater, they were gradually exposed as the lake evaporated to its present level.

Lake Tahoe sits high up in the snowy Sierra. All around it are slopes for downhill and cross-country skiing, snowboarding, and snowmobiling. On the lake itself, people enjoy scenic cruises in paddle wheelers and glass-bottomed boats.

The Central Valley

California's Central Valley is the richest, most productive farmland in the world. John Muir called it "one smooth, flowery, lake-like bed of fertile soil." Two rivers drain the long, narrow Central Valley: the Sacramento River in the north and the San Joaquin River in the south.

Just east of San Francisco Bay, around Stockton, the two rivers meet to form the Delta, a pleasantly tangled network of farming islands. Many people rent houseboats to explore the Delta and its river towns.

Fresno, in the center of the valley, is California's eighth-largest city. It's home to the nation's largest community of Hmong, a tribal people from Laos. One of Fresno's attractions is Chaffee Zoological Gardens. Rare snakes and lizards slink through natural habitats in the reptile exhibit. Meanwhile, tropical birds screech and dart through the tropical rain forest and Australian aviary.

Gold, rich farmland, and oil all helped to build Bakersfield. The town's Pioneer Village includes a museum and dozens of historic structures, such as a sheepherder's cabin, early oil-drilling rigs, and an old chuck wagon.

San Francisco

Fewer than 400 people lived in little Yerba Buena in 1845. Two years later, it had a new name— San Francisco. By 1860, the head count was 56,000. Sometimes sunny, sometimes cloaked in fog, San Francisco is now one of the most-visited cities in the country.

Visitors explore San Francisco on foot, by car, or aboard historic cable cars. Its streets follow the ups and downs of steep coastal hills. A landmark of Russian Hill is Lombard Street, the "world's crookedest street." It's famous for its eight hairpin curves and its terrifyingly steep slope.

In the foreground is one of San Francisco's famous cable cars; in the background is Alcatraz Island.

Nob Hill was once the home of railroad and silver barons. ("Nob" comes from *nabob*, an Urdu word for a big shot!) Its elegant hotels are a reminder of the city's Golden Age. Telegraph Hill is known for Coit Tower, a great lookout point for a view of the whole city.

San Francisco's fishing fleet still docks at Fisherman's Wharf, but crowds swarm to the waterfront for its shops and snack bars. Pier 39 has dozens of specialty shops. On its west side is a barking colony of sea lions. On the east side is UnderWater World. Here, visitors take a moving underwater walkway through a clear acrylic tunnel right under San Francisco Bay. The Marina District, built of rubble dumped there after the 1906 earthquake, became the site of the Panama-Pacific International Exposition in 1915. All the buildings except for the Palace of Fine Arts were torn down after the fair was over. From the hills behind the bay, the fashionable homes of Pacific Heights look down on the marina.

Around the Golden Gate Bridge are the grounds of the Presidio. First a Spanish fort, then a U.S. Army post, it's now part of the Golden Gate National Recreation Area—the world's largest national park in a city setting.

Golden Gate Park is full of brilliant rhododendrons and lush, prehistoric-looking tropical foliage. People stroll along walking trails or visit the arboretum and the exquisite Japanese Tea Garden. Nearby is the Asian Art Museum, which houses the largest collection of Asian art in the Western Hemisphere.

Downtown, the landmark Transamerica Pyramid towers over the financial district. The Civic Center complex includes City Hall, the library, and the symphony and opera halls. Dozens of movies have been filmed in City Hall's elegant interior.

Just west of the financial center is Chinatown. Established in the 1870s, it's now the city's most densely populated area, with about 20,000 residents. Magnificent dragons decorate the main entry on Grant Avenue. Beyond the gate, streets are jammed with import shops, jewelry stores, herbal medicine shops, restaurants, and garment factories.

North of Chinatown is City Lights Bookstore, a sort of cultural landmark. Jack Kerouac and other Beat-generation writers hung out there in the 1950s. Farther north is the Italian neighborhood of North Beach.

South of Market Street—called SoMa for short—is a trendy district of art galleries and outlet stores. The Mission District is named for Mission Dolores. Built in 1776, it's San Francisco's oldest building. The district's food markets and wall murals reflect its large Central American population.

San Francisco's Chinatown gate

The Castro District got its name from the ornate Castro Theater. Once a blue-collar neighborhood, it's now the center of San Francisco's gay community. Residents here started the Names Project and the AIDS Memorial Quilt to commemorate people who have died of AIDS (acquired immune deficiency syndrome).

In the 1960s, Haight-Ashbury was the hippie capital of the world. Janis Joplin, the Grateful Dead, Jefferson Airplane, and many other rock idols lived there.

Around the Bay Area

Ferries run from the mainland to Alcatraz Island. From 1934 to 1963, Alcatraz was a federal prison for such infamous gansters as Al Capone and George "Machine Gun" Kelly. Another ferry goes to mountainous, 740-acre (300-ha) Angel Island. Seals and sea lions lounge on its sandy beaches, and deer roam the woods.

Sather Tower at the University of California at Berkeley

North of San Francisco, across the Golden Gate Bridge, are the hills, mountains, and ocean scenery of Marin County. Sightseers enjoy driving or hiking through the deep redwood groves of Muir Woods.

Berkeley, which lies across from San Francisco on the East Bay, is the home of the University of California's most famous campus. Oakland is another East Bay city. Lake Merritt, right in the middle of town, is the world's largest saltwater tidal lake within a city. It's a pleasant spot for sailing, rowing, jogging, and wildlife watching. Fresh produce at bargain prices brings crowds to the farmers' market in Jack London Square. Oakland's Art Deco–style Paramount Theater once hosted Count Basie, Charlie Parker, and other jazz greats.

A scenic coastal drive south of San Francisco leads to Santa Cruz and its spectacular beach. Stanford University is in Palo Alto. Railroad magnate Leland Stanford and his wife built it in memory of their son who died of typhoid fever in 1884. San Jose, California's third-largest city, was once known for its fruit-tree orchards. Now it's the capital of Silicon Valley. Nearby Gilroy is proud to be the garlic capital of the world.

The TV series *Dynasty* was shot on Woodside's Filoli estate, the mansion and gardens of gold baron William Bourn. He named it after his favorite motto: FIght for a just cause, LOve your fellow man, LIve a good life.

The Central Coast

Small towns, rolling hills of wildflowers, and crashing surf on rugged shores—this is the coastline from San Francisco down to Los Angeles. Photographers Ansel Adams and Edward Weston recorded the beauty of the Central Coast in hundreds of dramatic black-and-white photos.

The Monterey Peninsula makes a crescent-shaped curve around Monterey Bay. The peninsula's 17-Mile Drive winds through pine forests and cypress groves, passing magnificent homes perched on the hillsides. The famous Lone Cypress grows out of a craggy cliff on the coast. This ancient, twisted tree is one of the most photographed sights in the state.

Local novelist John Steinbeck wrote about Monterey's Cannery Row in the days when it was the sardine-canning capital of the world. Now the canning warehouses are boutiques. Monterey Bay Aquarium is built out over the water at the end of the Row. The old mission town of Carmel is now officially called Carmel-by-the-Sea.

Ansel Adams often photographed California's central coast.

Clint Eastwood, Mayor

Actor, director, and producer Clint Eastwood (1930–) served as mayor of Carmel from 1986 to 1988. He was born Clinton Eastwood Jr. in San Francisco. After high school, he worked as a hay baler, a lumberjack, a honky-tonk piano player, and an army swimming instructor. After starring in the TV series *Rawhide*, he won international fame as the Man with No Name in Italian director Sergio Leone's "spaghetti Westerns" of the 1960s. Another famous role was the hard-nosed cop "Dirty Harry" Callahan, known for his famous line "Go ahead, make my day." Eastwood's haunting Western *Unforgiven* (1992) won him Oscars for best director and best picture. ■

Big Sur, a beautiful coastal strip that stretches from Carmel to San Simeon

This charming village attracts artists, writers, and people who want to escape fast city life.

Big Sur is the 90-mile (145-km) strip of coastline from Carmel to San Simeon. It's a scenic stretch of redwood forests and sheer granite ridges that drop to the sea. Highway 1, featured in many car commercials, snakes along the edge of the cliffs. Los Padres National Forest lines much of the Central Coast.

Farther inland is the fertile Salinas Valley. Called the "salad bowl of the world," it abounds in lettuce, tomatoes, garlic, and other vegetables. Salinas, the valley's major city, is best known as John Steinbeck's home. Outside of Salinas is San Juan Bautista. Its 1797 Spanish mission is still an active Catholic parish.

San Simeon's main attraction is Hearst Castle. Newspaperman William Randolph Hearst built it in the 1920s. Architect Julia Morgan designed the gardens, pools, terraces, and guest houses of the 123-acre (50-ha) estate. The "castle" itself is adorned with tapestries, giant-size fireplaces, and soaring columns.

Morro Rock, an extinct volcano, looms over Morro Bay. For Spanish explorers, it was a landmark visible far out at sea. Now peregrine falcons, cormorants, and pelicans nest in chinks in the rock. Father Junípero Serra founded the mission at nearby San Luis Obispo in 1772.

Pismo Beach is famous for two little creatures: the pismo clam and the monarch butterfly. Millions of migrating monarchs descend on the eucalyptus trees and Monterey pines every winter.

Santa Barbara began with Santa Barbara Mission and a presidio, the last Spanish fort built in the Americas. Downtown, buildings are restored in Spanish style with red-tile roofs, while bougainvillea blooms everywhere. Offshore are eight wild, overgrown islands called the Channel Islands. Five of them make up Channel Islands National Park.

Los Angeles

Olvera Street is the oldest street in Los Angeles. It's the main thoroughfare of the old city, El Pueblo de Los Angeles. There, the Mexican marketplace and historic buildings preserve the heritage of early Mexican settlers. Nearby, Little Tokyo and Chinatown showcase the city's Asian culture. Little Tokyo is the largest Japanese-American community in North America.

In the business district, some of the most beautiful buildings are the Museum of Contemporary Art, the Biltmore Hotel, and the Central Library. The pyramid-topped skyscraper of City Hall stands in the Civic Center area. Dorothy Chandler Pavilion is the home of the Los Angeles Philharmonic Orchestra and Los Angeles Opera. It also hosts the annual Academy Awards.

Wilshire Boulevard is Los Angeles's glitzy main thoroughfare. It continues west

Taking in the entertainment on Olvera Street, Los Angeles

Mann's Chinese Theater, where the sidewalks are studded with handprints and footprints of Hollywood stars.

through Beverly Hills, all the way to Santa Monica on the coast. Hancock Park, on Wilshire Boulevard, is the site of the La Brea Tar Pits, the Page Museum, and the Los Angeles County Museum of Art (LACMA). Spread out over five buildings, LACMA is the largest art museum in the western United States.

Exposition Park encloses the California Museum of Science and Industry, the Natural History Museum, the California Afro-American Museum, the Los Angeles Coliseum, and the Sports Arena. Nearby is the University of Southern California (USC), the oldest private university in the country.

North of downtown, in the Santa Monica Mountains, is Griffith Park—home of the Los Angeles Zoo and its 2,000 animals. But the best-known spot in the park is the famous "Hollywood" sign high on a hill. The Hollywood Bowl, the world's largest outdoor amphitheater, lies in a basin in the Santa Monica Mountains.

Hollywood, west of downtown Los Angeles, is the capital of the movie industry. In the 1930s and 1940s, the intersection of Hollywood and Vine was the center of Hollywood night life. Now tourists glimpse the past as they stroll down Hollywood Boulevard's Walk of Fame. Embedded in the sidewalks are more than 2,000 bronze stars, each with the name of a memorable Hollywood star. Handprints and footprints of the stars are immortalized in concrete in front of the landmark Mann's Chinese Theater.

West Hollywood is famous for Sunset Strip— the ten-block stretch of Sunset Boulevard from the 8200s through the 9200s. It's a hip strip of sidewalk cafés, discos, and famous clubs such as the Roxy and the Comedy Store.

Celebrities' mansions are everywhere in Beverly Hills and Bel Air. Tour buses take sightseers to see them. Some people visit Beverly Hills just to shop—or window-shop—along Rodeo Drive. This is a luxurious, three-block stretch of jewelry and designer-clothing boutiques.

The Los Angeles Area

Pasadena, in the San Gabriel Mountains northeast of Los Angeles, was once a winter resort. Now it's best known for the Rose Bowl and Tournament of Roses Parade on New Year's Day. Art museums in Pasadena are exceptional. Some of the best are the Huntington Art Gallery, the Norton Simon Museum of Art, and the Pacific-Asia Museum.

About one-third of Los Angeles's population lives in the San Fernando Valley. The valley's twenty-two adjoining towns are surrounded by the Santa Monica, San Gabriel, and Sierra Madre Mountains. Burbank, at the valley's eastern edge, is the home of NBC and Warner Brothers studios. Both give behind-the-scenes tours.

The San Fernando Valley, home to one-third of Los Angeles's residents

"Gag Me with a Spoon!"

"Duh! HEL-lo! He's like, grody to the max! And I'm like, gag me with a spoon! Totally tubular! Barf me out! I'm sure! As if!"

This is Valspeak, the dialect of the legendary Valley Girls, or Vals, who inhabit the San Fernando Valley. There, gangs of Vals hang out at the mall—say, the Galleria in Encino—getting their nails done and shopping for shoes. As with any cultural stereotype, the Valley Girl myth contains a grain of truth and a hearty dose of fiction.

Pop musician Frank Zappa immortalized Vals in his 1982 hit song "Valley Girl." Zappa's daughter, Moon Unit, supplied the nonstop Valley Girl rap vocals. Since the 1980s, Valspeak has become a nationwide language among young people. ■

Santa Monica is on the Pacific Coast directly west of Los Angeles. Santa Monica Pier, built in 1909, runs along the wide, sandy beach. People come from miles around to enjoy its restaurants, music clubs, and rides. Others enjoy the ocean views from the pier or from grassy Palisades Park.

Venice is just south of Santa Monica. It was meant to look like Venice, Italy, with canals and bridges, but the plan didn't get very far. Now Venice Beach is one of California's most popular beaches and people-watching spots. Rappers, jugglers, in-line skaters, and bodybuilders show themselves off daily along Oceanfront Walk.

Built in 1909, the Santa Monica Pier attracts people from miles around.

The rich and famous live up the coast in Malibu. This is a stretch of coast where the Santa Monica Mountains slope down to the sea. Besides a hot surfing beach, Malibu has the J. Paul Getty Museum. It houses the eccentric millionaire's art collection, including antiquities of ancient Greece and Rome.

South of Los Angeles is Long Beach. The retired ocean liner *Queen Mary* is docked at its harbor. Ferries run from here to Santa Catalina Island, 26 miles (42 km) offshore. Cars are not allowed on this wilderness island. Among the animals in its tangled interior is a large herd of wild buffalo.

Disneyland in Anaheim

Orange County

In the 1920s, Knott's Berry Farm was just a little roadside boysenberry stand in Buena Park. Now it's the oldest amusement park in the country, with more than 160 rides and shows. Other attractions in town are the Movieland Wax Museum, with 300 wax celebrities, and Ripley's Believe It or Not Museum.

In Anaheim, Mickey Mouse and his pals greet visitors to Disneyland. Also known as the Magic Kingdom, this world-famous theme park features eight theme "lands" and sixty adventure rides.

In Yorba Linda, northeast of Anaheim, is the Richard Nixon Library and Birthplace. Farther south is Mission San Juan Capis-

Walt Disney

Walter Elias Disney (1901–1966) was a pioneer in motion-picture animation. Disney's first Mickey Mouse cartoons appeared in 1928. His first feature-length films were *Snow White* (1937), *Pinocchio* (1938), and *Bambi* (1942). In 1955, Disney opened Disneyland, the world's first theme park, in Anaheim. A second park—Walt Disney World in Orlando, Florida—opened in 1971. Today, there are Disneyland theme parks in Europe and in Tokyo, Japan. ■

The Swallows of Capistrano

Father Junípero Serra built Mission San Juan de Capistrano, south of Anaheim, in 1776. An earthquake badly damaged the mission only a few years later. Since then, swallows have nested in the ruins. It's said that they leave on their winter migrations every October 23, the anniversary of St. John of Capistrano's death. Then they return every spring on March 19, St. Joseph's feast day. The swallows sometimes miss their schedule by a day or two, but they're close enough to keep the story—and the swallow-watchers—going. The legend inspired a popular 1940s tune, "When the Swallows Come Back to Capistrano." ■

trano. Founded in 1776, the mission is best known for the swallows that return every March.

Orange County's beaches attract surfers, boaters, and artists. The International Surfing Museum and the Surfing Hall of Fame are located in Huntington Beach. Farther down the coast, the popular spots are Newport Beach and Laguna Beach.

The Inland Empire

The farming region east of Los Angeles is called the Inland Empire. Riverside, its major city, was one of the wealthiest cities in the nation in the 1890s. Thousands of acres of orange groves stretched to the horizon. Riverside's Mission Inn, Heritage House, and City Hall preserve the town's days of glory. In nearby Redlands stand the 300 Marmalade Mansions. They're the restored Victorian homes of citrus kings.

A reservoir near Hemet is called the Valley of the Mastodons. In 1997, researchers there discovered a treasure trove of Ice Age fossils.

The scenic Rim of the World Drive winds through the forested San Bernardino Mountains. It leads to sparkling Big Bear Lake, Arrowhead Lake, and many popular ski slopes. At the foot of the mountains is the city of San Bernardino. It's the county seat of San Bernardino County and one of the state's major agricultural areas.

Other sights in the area are the olive canneries in Ontario, the Los Angeles County Fair in Pomona, and the Wigwam Village Motel. This relic of the 1940s offered tepee-shaped motel rooms to travelers on Route 66.

In the lush Imperial Valley, El Centro and Brawley are the major towns. The valley blooms—thanks to irrigation canals from the Colorado River.

The Mission Inn at Riverside

The Deserts

California's deserts offer a panorama of colored canyons, wind-sculpted rocks, and desolate, windswept dunes. But they're alive, too, with small, scurrying creatures, wildflowers, towering cacti, and prickly trees. In some places, the scorching heat could fry an egg. Elsewhere, palm trees wave in the warm breeze over oases where precious water gushes from the ground.

Death Valley National Monument is one of the hottest places on the planet. Zabriskie Point and Dante's View are favorite lookout points over the whole region. Below Death Valley, the Mojave Desert covers a vast area of southeastern California, spilling over into Nevada. On the west edge of the desert is Edwards Air Force Base, a landing site for space shuttles.

Moviemakers love the surrounding landscape. Red Rock Canyon was the filming site for *Jurassic Park*. Nearby Trona Pinnacles, with hundreds of volcanic tufa towers, provided the set for *Star Trek V* and other space movies.

Barstow is the main town in the Mojave and the crossroads of several highways. A stretch of old Route 66 runs between Essex and Ludlow. It's like a graveyard, with ghostly old gas stations and diners left from the 1940s.

Palm Springs boasts many golf courses, including the Desert Princess.

Ghost towns are all that's left from the Mojave's silver mines of the nineteenth century. At Silver King Mine, people can explore the old mines through miles of tunnels. The ghost town of Calico is now restored with 1880s shops and even fake gunfights. Calico's Early Man Site is an archaeological dig where ancient stone tools have been found.

Palm Springs spreads out in the Coachella Valley beneath the San Jacinto Mountains. Cahuilla Indians lived there when Juan Bautista de Anza stumbled along in 1774. It was a welcome sight when he found steamy water bubbling from the ground. The waters and the dry desert air lured people there for their health. In the 1930s, developers built Palm Springs into a luxurious resort.

Joshua Tree National Monument is a short drive from Palm Springs. At Blythe, near the Arizona border, Indians have carved gigantic figures on the ground.

San Diego

Mission San Diego de Alcalá, California's first mission, was built on San Diego's Presidio Hill. Now only its ruins remain. Friars relocated the mission a few miles away, where it stands today. Now the Junípero Serra Museum commands a sweeping view from atop Presidio Hill.

Down the hill is Old Town San Diego, a cluster of Spanish-style gardens and shops. In the downtown area are the historic Gaslamp Quarter and Horton Plaza shopping center. The Embarcadero, a walkway along the waterfront, offers a view of ships and seagulls.

Hippo Beach, Monkey Mesa, and Gorilla Tropics are some of the true-to-life animal habitats at San Diego Zoo. The world-famous zoo in Balboa Park is home to about 4,000 animals. Some of the exotic residents are wild Mongolian horses, fierce Indonesian Komodo dragons, New Zealand kiwis, Australian koalas, and the giant pandas Shi Shi and Bai Yun.

One of the giant pandas at the San Diego Zoo

Sea World of California is part of a gigantic park along Mission Bay. Its biggest attraction is the killer whale stunt show.

Across San Diego Bay from the city is Coronado Peninsula. Visitors gather seashells along the beach or tour the Hotel del Coronado. This grand old resort hotel has appeared in many movies. L. Frank Baum, a local resident, wrote *The Wizard of Oz*. It's said that he modeled the story's Emerald City after the Coronado hotel.

Far out on a peninsula is Cabrillo National Monument, honoring the explorer's arrival in California in 1542. Just south of San Diego, across the Mexican border, is Tijuana. Called TJ for short, Tijuana gets more tourists than any other Mexican border town.

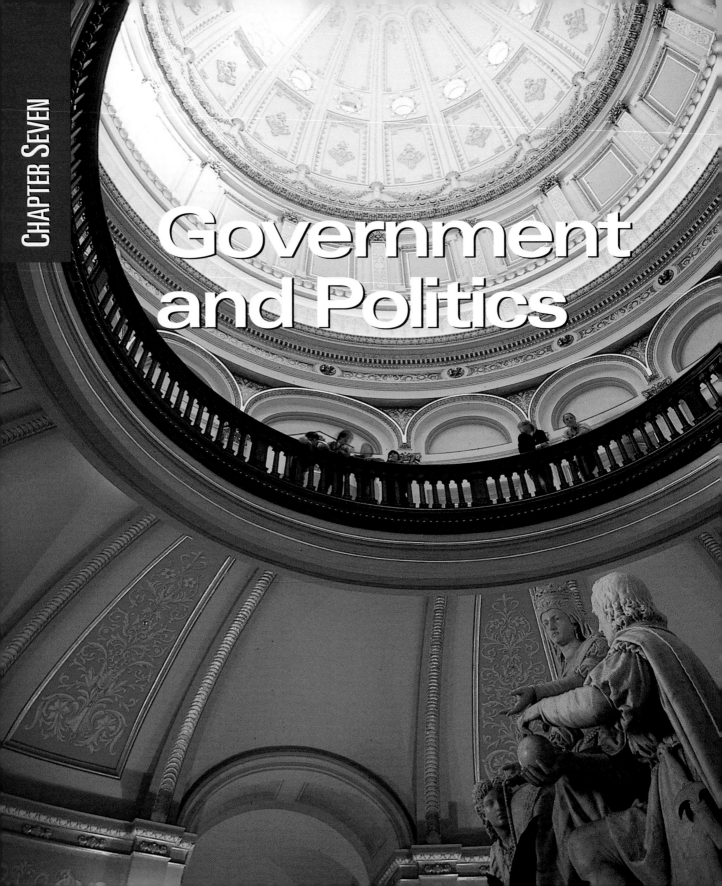

Government and Politics

Californians have a long history of taking the law into their own hands. Back in the Gold Rush days, mining camps worked out their own rules for exploring, staking claims, and keeping order. Vigilance committees took a meaner turn. They exiled or even hanged people they couldn't tolerate. Today, citizens have a more civilized way of taking control. When they want a direct voice in the lawmaking process, they use the initiative or the referendum.

For an initiative, 5 percent of the voters sign a petition to put a measure on the ballot in the next election. Citizens can also use the initiative to propose an amendment, or change, to the state constitution. In that case, the petition has to be signed by 8 percent of the voters.

If the citizens don't like a law that the legislature passed, they can use the referendum. Here, if 5 percent of the voters challenge the law, it won't go into effect until people vote on it in the next election.

Opposite: The dome
ceiling in the state
capitol building

The State Constitution—
Time to Reexamine

California adopted its first constitution in 1849, when it was still a territory. Among other things, it gave married women the right to their own property. In many other states, the husband owned his wife's property as soon as they married. That document stayed in force until 1879, when the present-day constitution was adopted. Since then, more than 350 amendments, or changes, have been added to the basic document.

In the 1990s, state officials couldn't help noticing the high number of voter initiatives that passed every year. They concluded that Californians were frustrated with the way their government works. From 1994 to 1996, a constitutional review commission met to examine the state government. The commission made a number of proposals to help the government run more efficiently and serve the people better.

The basic structure of California's state government is a good one. It will probably stay the same. It's organized just like the federal government in Washington, D.C. Ruling power is shared among three branches of government: executive, legislative, and judicial. The three divisions keep a check on one another, so that there's always a balance of power.

The Executive Branch

The executive branch of government sees that the state laws are carried out. The governor is the state's chief executive and the head of the executive branch. Voters elect a governor to serve up to two four-year terms. They also elect the lieutenant governor, who is sec-

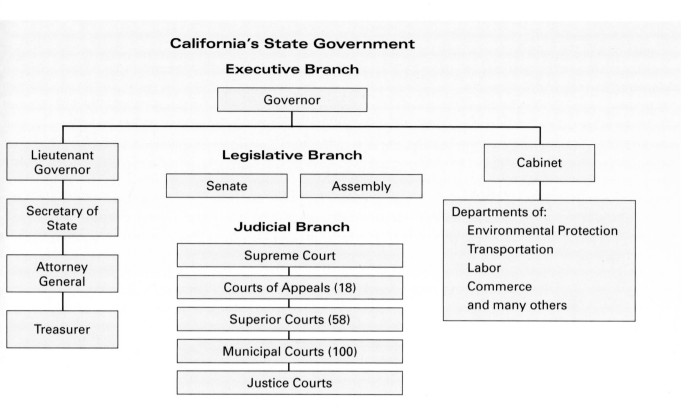

California's State Government

Executive Branch

Governor

Lieutenant Governor

Secretary of State

Attorney General

Treasurer

Legislative Branch

Senate

Assembly

Judicial Branch

Supreme Court

Courts of Appeals (18)

Superior Courts (58)

Municipal Courts (100)

Justice Courts

Cabinet

Departments of:
Environmental Protection
Transportation
Labor
Commerce
and many others

ond in command. The lieutenant governor is president of the Senate but votes only to break a tie.

Several other executive officers are chosen by the state's voters. The secretary of state keeps records of official government acts and watches over elections. The attorney general is the state's chief law enforcement officer, making sure the state laws are enforced in every county. The state treasurer is the state's banker, who watches over the state treasury and reports on funds going in and out. All are limited to two terms in office.

The governor appoints cabinet members, or advisers, to head eight major state agencies. These agencies oversee areas such as health and welfare, environmental protection, and housing.

The Legislature

The state legislature's job is to make state laws. California's legislature is modeled after the U.S. Congress. It is composed of two houses, or chambers: the State Senate and the State Assembly. Senators and Assembly members are elected from districts that are mapped out according to the number of residents. Every ten years, the districts are remapped to account for shifts in the population.

California's forty state senators are elected to four-year terms and can serve up to two terms. The state Assembly is like the house of representatives in most other states. The eighty Assembly members serve up to three terms of two years each.

The legislature comes to order on the first Monday in December of even-numbered years. Each regular session lasts two years, ending on November 30 of the next even-numbered year. The governor may also call special sessions to deal with specific problems.

The Judicial Branch

California's judicial system is one of the largest in the world. Judges in the state courts make up the judicial branch of government. Their job is to interpret the law. When they rule on a case, they use state laws, previous decisions, and the state constitution to make their decision.

California's Supreme Court is the state's highest court. It consists of a chief justice and six associate justices, each serving a twelve-year term. The governor appoints them, a judicial commission confirms the appointments, and the public gives the final approval at the next election. The Supreme Court regularly meets in San Francisco, Los Angeles, and Sacramento.

Supreme Court judges spend most of their time reviewing cases appealed from a lower court. They decide important legal questions and settle arguments about whether a lower court made the right decision. By law, they must also review all cases in which the defendant was given the death penalty. All the other state courts must abide by the Supreme Court's decisions.

Lower Courts

Under the Supreme Court are courts of appeal, superior courts, municipal courts, and justice courts. The courts of appeal are panels of three judges each. Mostly they hear appeals from the superior courts. California has six appeals court districts, with eighteen divisions and eighty-eight judges.

Serious criminal and civil trials take place in California's superior courts. Each of the fifty-eight counties has a superior court, but each court may have many judges. Los Angeles County's superior court, for example, has more than 200 judges. Statewide, there are 789 superior court judges. Like the Supreme Court justices, they are appointed by the governor and approved by the voters. They serve six-year terms.

California's superior courts hear more than a million cases a year. About one-fourth of the cases are criminal cases, and the rest are civil.

Each county is divided into judicial districts. As soon as a district has more than 40,000 residents, it gets a municipal court. Smaller districts have justice courts. Judges in these courts serve six-year terms. They hear criminal misdemeanor cases and civil cases involving $25,000 or less.

The entrance to California's Supreme Court

California's Governors

Name	Party	Term	Name	Party	Term
Peter H. Burnett	Dem.	1849–1851	Henry T. Gage	Rep.	1899–1903
John McDougal	Dem.	1851–1852	George C. Pardee	Rep.	1903–1907
John Bigler	Dem.	1852–1856	James N. Gillett	Rep.	1907–1911
John Neely Johnson		1856–1858	Hiram W. Johnson	Rep.	1911–1917
John B. Weller	Dem.	1858–1860	William D. Stephens	Rep.	1917–1923
Milton S. Latham	Dem.	1860	Friend William Richardson	Rep.	1923–1927
John G. Downey	Dem.	1860–1862			
Leland Stanford	Rep.	1862–1863	Clement C. Young	Rep.	1927–1931
Frederick F. Low	Union	1863–1867	James Rolph Jr.	Rep.	1931–1934
Henry H. Haight	Dem.	1867–1871	Frank F. Merriam	Rep.	1934–1939
Newton Booth	Rep.	1871–1875	Culbert L. Olson	Dem.	1939–1943
Romualdo Pacheco	Rep.	1875	Earl Warren	Rep.	1943–1953
William Irwin	Dem.	1875–1880	Goodwin J. Knight	Rep.	1953–1959
George C. Perkins	Rep.	1880–1883	Edmund G. Brown	Dem.	1959–1967
George Stoneman	Dem.	1883–1887	Ronald Reagan	Rep.	1967–1975
Washington Bartlett	Dem.	1887	Edmund G. Brown Jr.	Dem.	1975–1983
Robert W. Waterman	Rep.	1887–1891	George Deukmejian	Rep.	1983–1991
Henry H. Markham	Rep.	1891–1895	Pete Wilson	Rep.	1991–
James H. Budd	Dem.	1895–1899			

How an Idea Becomes Law

Every law starts out as an idea, and any citizen—even children—can bring up an idea for a law. The first step is to persuade a member of the legislature to sponsor the idea. If the legislator agrees to take it on, he or she has the proposal written up properly. Then it officially becomes a bill. It's introduced at the Senate or Assembly desk (depending on the sponsor's house). There, the bill is given a number and read for the first time.

Then the bill goes directly to the rules committee, which sends it to a policy committee. These committees specialize in certain areas such as agriculture, health, or transportation.

Dianne Feinstein

Dianne Feinstein (1933–) was born in San Francisco. In 1969, she joined San Francisco's Board of Supervisors, serving three terms as its president.

After Mayor George Moscone was assassinated in 1978, she became the city's first woman mayor, serving until 1988. In 1992, Feinstein became California's first woman U.S. senator. She was elected to a six-year term in 1994, taking seats on the senate's foreign relations, judiciary, and rules committees.

Feinstein, a Democrat, is known for her tough stands against gangs, drugs, and crime. ■

When it's time for a hearing, the committee listens to testimony from people who are for and against the measure. If the law would cost the state money, a fiscal committee also hears testimony. Not many people realize that most bills "die" at the committee stage.

If the bill survives the committees, it goes to the house members for debate and a vote. Once it passes in the house of origin, the bill goes to the other house, where the committee process begins anew. If the second house amends, or changes, the bill, the house of origin must agree to the changes before the bill can move on.

After both houses pass the bill, it goes to the governor. The governor has twelve days to sign the bill into law or veto it. It takes a two-thirds vote in both houses of the legislature to overturn the veto.

Earl Warren

Earl Warren (1891–1974), born in Los Angeles, was district attorney of Alameda County (Oakland) and state attorney general. He was elected governor of California in 1942 and reelected twice. In 1948, Warren ran for vice-president with Republican presidential candidate Thomas E. Dewey. In 1953, President Dwight D. Eisenhower appointed Warren chief justice of the U.S. Supreme Court. He retired in 1969. Warren, a political liberal, presided over many important decisions, such as outlawing racial segregation in public schools. ■

California's State Symbols

State flower: Golden poppy Golden poppies (above) grow wild all over the state. They're also called flame flowers, as well as the Italian names *la amapola* (poppy) and *copo d'oro* (cup of gold). April 6 is California Poppy Day.

State tree: California redwood Towering redwoods once covered much of the Northern Hemisphere. Today they're found only near the Pacific coast. There are two species. The sierra redwoods grow in the Sierra Nevada Mountains. Their trunks are the most enormous in the world, with some measuring 35 feet (11 m) across. Coast redwoods—the world's tallest trees—grow along California's central and northern coasts and Oregon's southern coast.

State animal: California grizzly bear California's last grizzly bear died in 1922. Before that, grizzlies played an important role in California's history. Settlers and rancheros hunted them for food. Revolutionaries in Sonoma used the grizzly on their flag as a territorial symbol. Today, the same California grizzly bear appears on the state flag.

State bird: California valley quail The California valley quail is a plump gray game bird found throughout the state. On top of its head is a black plume of feathers. Under its beak is a black bib with a white stripe. Quails travel in flocks, but in the spring, they pair off and mate. The nest is a hollow in the ground, where the female quail lays up to twenty-eight cream-colored eggs with brown spots.

State fish: South Fork golden trout The South Fork golden trout is a brilliantly colored species of trout. It lives only in the icy waters of the South Fork of the Kern River in the High Sierra. It's a small fish, averaging about 8 inches (20 cm) long.

State reptile: California desert tortoise California desert tortoises (below) live longer than humans and longer than any other vertebrate. They are found in California's deserts and grow up to 12 inches (30 cm) long. Because they are disappearing, desert tortoises are protected. It's against the law to take them from their natural habitat.

State insect: California dog-face butterfly In 1929, entomologists (scientists who study insects) all over the state voted to pick the state insect. The dog-face butterfly won. The male is orange with black wing borders, and the female is yellow-orange with a black spot on each upper wing. The two spots look like the two eyes of a dog. The butterfly is only about 2 inches (5 cm) across. It lives from the San Francisco area down to San Diego.

State mineral: Native gold Gold gave California its nickname, the Golden State. This glistening mineral inspired the Gold Rush of 1849. California is still one of the top gold-producing states in the nation. And some California mining sites let visitors pan for gold.

State rock: Serpentine California has more of this green-and-blue rock than any other state. Used in making asbestos, serpentine contains the minerals chromite, magnesite, and cinnabar. California was the first state to name an official state rock when it chose serpentine in 1965.

State gemstone: Benitoite Called the "blue diamond," this rare gem was first discovered in the San Benito River. Its color ranges from pale blue to dark sapphire blue.

State marine mammal: California gray whale In the fall, California gray whales (above, right) can be seen migrating south along the California shore. They're on their way from Alaska's Bering Sea to Baja California, where they mate and have their calves. In the spring, they head north again. Each trip covers as much as 7,000 miles (11,265 km). Gray whales measure 35 to 50

feet (11 to 15 m) and weigh 20 to 40 tons.

State fossil: Saber-toothed cat Short-legged and muscular with a stubby tail, saber-toothed cats were larger than modern lions. Their deadly fangs were 8 inches (20 cm) long. Many specimens were preserved in Los Angeles's La Brea Tar Pits.

The State Flag

California's state flag is called the Bear Flag. It features a red star and a grizzly bear on a white background. Underneath are the words "California Republic" and a red band. Grizzlies were common creatures in the wilds of California. The star was an imitation of the "lone star" of the Texas flag. William Todd made the first Bear Flag on a piece of unbleached cotton cloth. In the Bear Flag Revolt of June 14, 1846, settlers took over the Mexican headquarters at Sonoma. They raised the Bear Flag and declared California an independent republic. After statehood in 1850, the American flag flew over California. The Bear Flag was declared the state flag in 1911.

California's State Song
"I Love You, California"

Words by F. B. Silverwood   Music by A. F. Frankenstein

I love you, California, you're the
greatest state of all;
I love you in the winter, summer, spring, and in fall;
I love your fertile valleys; your
dear mountains I adore;
I love your grand old ocean,
and I love her rugged shore.

Chorus:
Where the snow-crowned
Golden Sierras
Keep their watch o'er the val-
leys' bloom,
It is there I would be, in our land
by the sea,
Ev'ry breeze bearing rich per-
fume,

It is here nature gives of her
rarest.
It is Home Sweet Home to me,
And I know when I die, I shall
breathe my last sigh
For my sunny California.

I love your redwood forests—
love your fields of yellow
grain;
I love your summer breezes,
and I love your winter rain;
I love you, land of flowers; land
of honey, fruit, and wine;
I love you, California; you have
won this heart of mine.

(Chorus)

I love your old gray missions—
love your vineyards stretch-
ing far;
I love you, California, with your
Golden Gate ajar;
I love your purple sunsets, love
your skies of azure blue;
I love you, California; I just can't
help loving you.
(Chorus)
I love you, California, you are
very dear to me;
I love you, Tamalpais, and I love
Yosemite;
I love you, land of sunshine,
half your beauties are untold;
I loved you in my childhood, and
I'll love you when I'm old.

Local Government and Home Rule

Most of California's fifty-eight counties are governed by a five-member board of supervisors. Voters elect them, along with several other county officers. These usually include a sheriff, county clerk, assessor, district attorney, and school superintendent. In 1998, California had 470 incorporated cities. Most cities elect a mayor or city manager as their chief executive and a city council as their legislature.

According to the state constitution, cities and counties may choose to have home rule. This means that they can draw up their

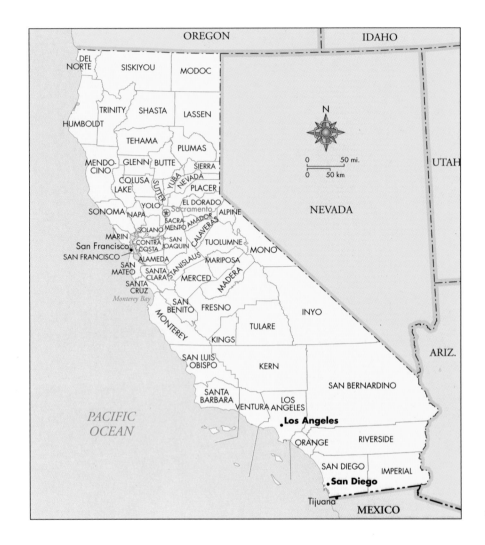

California's counties

own charter—something like their own local constitution. Such a plan gives local communities more power to govern their own affairs. Any city with a population of more than 3,500 is entitled to home rule. However, only about eighty cities have their own charters. Of the fifty-eight counties, eleven have chosen home rule.

CHAPTER EIGHT

A Wealthy State

Back in the 1850s, Californians threatened to declare their state a separate country. If they had, they would have done just fine. If California were a country today, it would have one of the richest economies in the world.

In 1996, California's gross state product (GSP) was $962.1 billion. (The gross state product is the total value of all the goods and services the state produces in a year.) That's not only the highest GSP in the nation, it's one of the ten-highest outputs in the world, outranking the countries of Canada, Mexico, and Russia. In fact, almost 3 percent of the entire world's production comes from California! By 1998, California's GSP was estimated to be over $1 trillion.

Why is California so incredibly rich? It starts with natural resources: plenty of sunshine, minerals galore, great soils, water for irrigation, and a year-round growing season in much of the state.

Add to that the people factor. Lavish resources and a wonderful climate attract people and businesses. With the country's highest population, California has a solid supply of labor at all levels, from farm and factory workers to high-tech scientists.

Service industries account for 77 percent of California's GSP. Service workers hold a wide range of jobs. They include Holly-

The vineyards of Napa Valley contribute to California's rich economy.

Opposite: The Los Angeles skyline as seen from Echo Park

Universal Studios

Filmmaker Carl Laemmle bought a chicken farm in 1915 and built a couple of movie sets on it. There he filmed the first open-air silent films. For twenty-five cents' admission, Laemmle gave tours and explained how movies were made. Laemmle's chicken farm is now Universal Studios, and people pay a lot more to get in. But the tours are just as fascinating now as they were then.

This 420-acre (170-ha) film studio is the largest in the world. More than 500 outdoor sets re-create the look of Wild West towns, European cities, Mexican villages, New York City, and other locations.

On the backlot tram tour, visitors from around the world watch avalanches, earthquakes, explosions, and fires. They're accosted by the shark from *Jaws* and 33-foot (10-m) King Kong. ◼

Date palms in California's Imperial Valley

wood actors and directors, doctors and nurses, real estate salespeople, gas station clerks, schoolteachers, and truck drivers.

Farming

Whether you're having breakfast, lunch, or dinner, you're probably eating something from California. The state grows 55 percent of the nation's fruits, nuts, and vegetables. Almost all the almonds, pistachios, walnuts, kiwi fruits, olives, and dates in the country come from California. If you add up the value of all U.S. crops, you'll find that California produces one-eighth of the total.

Ask anyone to name the nation's top dairy state, and they'll probably say Wisconsin. Wrong! It's California. Milk and cream are the state's leading farm products, with grapes ranking second. Vineyards in the Sonoma and Napa Valleys make some of the finest wines in the world. California leads the nation in cut flowers, potted plants, shrubs, and other decorative plants. San Diego County is the center for these greenhouse and nursery products.

California Farm Facts

- 29 percent of California's total land area is farmland.

- Average farm size: 373 acres (151 ha)

- Number of farms: About 80,000

- Top-ten farm products: milk and cream, grapes, nursery and greenhouse products, cattle and calves, cotton, almonds, hay, lettuce, flowers and foliage, and tomatoes

- California is the nation's top exporter of food. It goes to Pacific Rim countries (55 percent), Canada (18 percent), Europe (9 percent), and Mexico (5 percent). California exports the most vegetables, fruits, and nuts.

- Top six agricultural counties: Fresno, Tulare, Kern, Monterey, Merced, and San Joaquin

- California ranks first in the production of more than seventy-five farm products.

- Almost all (99 percent or more) of these U.S. crops come from California: almonds, artichokes, dates, figs, kiwi fruit, olives, persimmons, pistachios, prunes, raisins, clovers, and walnuts.

- 91 percent of the nation's grape crop and 72 percent of its lettuce (right) comes from California.

- California has been the number-one farming state for more than fifty years in a row.

Cesar Chávez

Cesar Estrada Chávez (1927–1993) was an activist in the National Farm Workers Association labor union. In 1962, he convinced California's Mexican-American farmworkers to join the union. Chávez led a nation-wide boycott of California grapes and lettuce in 1965. This won collective bargaining rights for the farmworkers. Their union became the United Farm Workers of America in 1973. ∎

Fresno County, right in the middle of the Central Valley, is the top-ranking agricultural county—not just in California, but in the whole nation. Its farmers raise a great variety of products: grapes, cotton, tomatoes, garlic, peaches, nectarines, cantaloupes, and turkeys.

The Salinas Valley in Monterey County is salad territory. Its huge farms make California number one in cauliflower and broccoli, as well as artichokes, spinach, lettuce, and other salad greens. Thanks to the orange groves in Tulare and Kern counties, California is second only to Florida in orange production.

Gazpacho

California's bounty of fresh vegetables is the basis for this delicious and cool summer soup.

Ingredients:

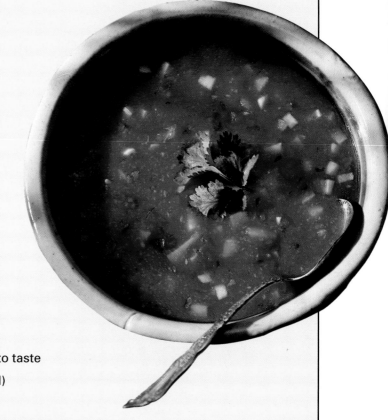

     6 large ripe tomatoes, preferably
       ripened on the vine

     1 red pepper, diced

     1 yellow pepper, diced

     1 large Spanish onion, chopped

     2 celery stalks, chopped

     2 large shallots, chopped

     2 large cucumbers, peeled,
       seeded, and chopped

     2 ripe, but still fairly firm, avocados,
       peeled, seeded, and chopped

  1 3/4 cups of canned tomato juice

     4 tablespoons of fresh cilantro

   1/2 clove of garlic, pressed

   1/4 cup of extra virgin olive oil

     1 tablespoon of lemon juice

       a dash of red wine vinegar, or more to taste

       a dash of hot sauce to taste (optional)

       salt and black pepper to taste

       garlic croutons and fresh cilantro for garnish

Directions:

Core the tomatoes, trying to save the juice.

In a large bowl, mix the fresh tomato juice, the canned juice, the cilantro, the garlic, the olive oil, the lemon juice, and the vinegar.

In a blender, puree the tomatoes and the other vegetables, pouring in some of the tomato juice mixture occasionally, to keep the vegetables from sticking to the blades of the blender. Try not to puree the vegetables for too long; the mixture should be chunky.

Add the vegetable mixture to the tomato sauce, stir, and add hot sauce, salt, and pepper.

Cover the bowl, and chill in the refrigerator for at least six hours.

Serve in chilled bowls or glasses, with garlic croutons and a little fresh cilantro on top.

Steven Jobs

Steven Paul Jobs (1955–) was born in Los Altos. He grew up in Mountain View surrounded by apricot orchards and graduated from Cupertino's Homestead High School in 1972. In his family's garage, he and Steve Wozniak, another Homestead graduate, started a computer company. They named it Apple, after Jobs's favorite fruit. The two designed the Apple II computer in 1977. Three years later, Apple became a public corporation, and the two Steves became instant millionaires. Pixar, Jobs's computer animation company, made *Toy Story* (1995), the third-highest-grossing animated film of all time. Jobs lives in Silicon Valley with his wife and three children. ■

Manufacturing

Every time you see a space shuttle blast off, you're watching a California product. Most of the spacecraft for the nation's space program come from factories around Los Angeles. Military and commercial aircraft are another specialty. More airplanes roll off the assembly lines in southern California than anywhere else in the country. California also gets more contracts to build military equipment than any other state.

California is the nation's top manufacturing state. Manufacturing accounts for about one-seventh of California's GSP. The most valuable factory goods are aircraft, spacecraft, cars, and other vehicles. Next in importance are processed foods and electronic equipment.

Much of California's food crop goes straight from the farm to the processing plant. Fruits and vegetables are canned, and oranges are turned into juice. Wheat makes its way to bakeries, and grapes ferment into wine.

What California Grows, Manufactures, and Mines

Agriculture	Manufacturing	Mining
Milk and cream	Transportation equipment	Petroleum
Grapes	Food products	Natural gas
Greenhouse and nursery products	Electrical equipment	
Beef cattle	Machinery	

Chances are good that your computer was made in California. IBM, Apple, Hewlett Packard, Intel, Netscape, and dozens of other computer firms saturate San Jose and surrounding communities. During the computer boom of the 1960s, the region got the name Silicon Valley, after the silicon chips used in computer circuits.

Mining

If you head out to California with a pick and a pan, could you find gold? Yes! Some geologists say that 70 percent of the gold that was in Gold Country in 1849 is still there. Many sites in the region offer gold-panning expeditions on the rivers. You may not strike it rich, but it's not unusual for amateurs to find gold flecks glistening in the bottom of their pans.

California is still one of the top gold-producing states. But the most valuable mineral in California today is "black gold"—petroleum. Petroleum (oil) and natural gas bring in about three-fourths of California's mining income.

After fuels, industrial minerals are the most important. California ranks first in sodium sulfate, construction sand and gravel, and portland cement. Practically all the boron and asbestos in the

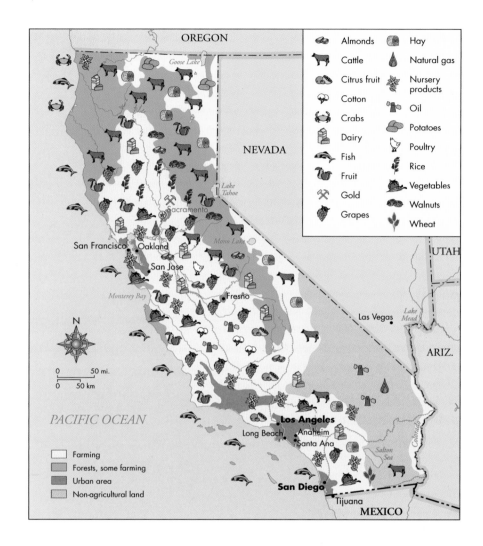

California's natural resources

Map legend:
- Almonds
- Cattle
- Citrus fruit
- Cotton
- Crabs
- Dairy
- Fish
- Fruit
- Gold
- Grapes
- Hay
- Natural gas
- Nursery products
- Oil
- Potatoes
- Poultry
- Rice
- Vegetables
- Walnuts
- Wheat

- Farming
- Forests, some farming
- Urban area
- Non-agricultural land

United States comes from California. Boron is used to make boric acid, an eyewash, and borax, a cleanser.

California is the only state that produces tungsten, which is used in electronics. It's also one of the top producers of gypsum, magnesium, molybdenum, feldspar, and pumice. California is first in the production of diatomite—a grainy, chalklike mineral that builds up on ocean floors. It's formed by the shells of tiny algae called diatoms.

Mining is valuable to California's economy, but it causes problems, too. Open-pit mines tear up the landscape, and mining near streams pollutes the water. At Iron Mountain near Redding, abandoned copper mines constantly leak copper and acids into the Sacramento River. High levels of toxic copper have been found in clams in San Francisco Bay. Many applications for mining permits are denied out of concern for the environment. Local governments often require mining companies to clean up or restore the land.

Fishing

Fresh seafood is one of California's finest taste treats. From shark and swordfish to shrimp and squid, California's coastal waters yield a rich harvest. California catches more tuna than any other state. Other important catches include rockfish, halibut, salmon, and shellfish such as abalone and crabs. Squid, eaten as fried or boiled calamari, is so popular that fishermen worry about the supplies disappearing.

Transportation

El Camino Real—the Royal Road—once linked California's missions from San Diego up to Sonoma. Now Route 5 and U.S. Highway 101 follow roughly the same route. State Highway 1, the scenic drive along the coast, runs from Los Angeles all the way up to the northern redwood country.

Old westward trails into California are now modern interstate highways. Interstate 40 used to be legendary Route 66. From 1926

A catch of oysters at Hog Island

to 1985, Route 66 paved the way from Chicago to Los Angeles—2,400 miles (3,860 km). Once in California, motorists were greeted with diners, orange-shaped juice stands, and wigwam-shaped motels.

Good roads reach almost every part of the state. California maintains 170,383 miles (274,205 km) of public streets, roads, and highways. The state's first freeway, the Arroyo Seco Parkway, opened in 1940. Renamed the Pasadena Freeway, it runs between Pasadena and Los Angeles. Today, the Los Angeles Freeway is famous for two things: high-speed motorists and snail's-pace traffic jams.

It's expensive to own a car in California. Fees for registration and emissions tests, or "smog checks," are high. Public transportation systems in Los Angeles and San Francisco include both buses and a network of trains.

Andrew Hallidie, a Scottish immigrant, designed San Francisco's cable cars in 1872. Electrified since the early 1900s, they're still running today. The entire system is a national historic landmark, with twenty-eight cars scaling 4.5 miles (7.2 km) of city streets.

When John Frémont saw the entrance to San Francisco Bay, it reminded him of another strait—the Golden Horn leading to Istanbul, Turkey. On the spot, he named the California site the Golden Gate. The Golden Gate Bridge, opened in 1937, carries 100,000 vehicles a day between San Francisco and Marin County. It glistens in the afternoon sun with its 5,000-gallon (18,926-l) coat of orange paint.

The Oakland Bay Bridge spans the bay between San Francisco and Oakland. It's a double-decker, with traffic running on

The legendary Route 66 ran from Chicago to Los Angeles.

The Oakland Bay Bridge is one of the longest bridges in the world.

upper and lower levels. At 5.2 miles (8.4 km) long, it's one of the longest bridges in the world.

California is a prime spot for testing experimental aircraft. For commercial flights, international airports serve Los Angeles and San Francisco. International passengers land at Oakland, San Diego, and San Jose, too. Dozens of other cities have airports that handle domestic flights.

Los Angeles, Long Beach, San Diego, and San Francisco have major ports that handle container ships with international cargo. In San Francisco Bay, there are several deepwater ports: San Francisco, Oakland, Redwood City, and Richmond. Farm products and minerals travel down the Sacramento and San Joaquin rivers to Sacramento and Stockton. From there, deepwater channels enable heavy ships to carry the cargo down to San Francisco Bay.

Communication

California's first newspaper, *The Californian*, first came out in Monterey in 1846. A year later, the *California Star* appeared in Yerba Buena—the town that became San Francisco. Sam Brannan, the *Star*'s publisher, gets credit for starting the Gold Rush. His headlines were the first to declare the news of Marshall's gold find in Coloma.

Literary journals were popular in early California. *Golden Era* and *The Overland Monthly* published early works by Mark Twain, Ambrose Bierce, and Bret Harte.

Today, the *Los Angeles Times* and the *San Francisco Chronicle* are the state's biggest newspapers. Other major daily papers are the *San Francisco Examiner*, *San Diego Union-Tribune*, *Sacramento Bee*, *Orange County Register*, and *San Jose Mercury News*. Some important monthly periodicals are *California Magazine*, *Los Angeles Magazine*, and *San Francisco Magazine*.

Stockton's KWG radio station, launched in 1921, is still broadcasting. KTLA, the state's first TV station, started up in Los Angeles in 1947. Now, about 685 radio stations and 90 TV stations are operating in the state. About 64 percent of California households have cable TV.

Breaking the Sound Barrier

No one thought it was possible to fly faster than Mach 1, the speed of sound. But Chuck Yaeger (above) proved them wrong. In October 1947, Yaeger broke the sound barrier in the skies over what would later be Edwards Air Force Base. He flew an X-1 aircraft he named *Glamorous Glennis*, after his wife. On the ground, sound travels at about 700 miles (1,127 km) per hour. At Yaeger's altitude of 40,000 feet (12,192 m), sound travels slower—at about 660 miles (1,062 km) per hour. ■

CHAPTER NINE

The Faces of California

About one out of every eight people in the United States is a Californian. In 1995, California's population was roughly 31.6 million. Texas, with the next highest population, was far behind with 18.7 million. California is not only the most populous state in the Union, but it also gets the most new residents every year.

No other developed area in the world has grown as fast as California. From 1900 to 1950, the population grew from 1.5 million people to 10.5 million. Over the next forty years, 1950 to 1990, the population almost tripled again. From 1980 to 1990, the population increased by more than 25 percent. The growth rate has slowed down since 1990, but experts expect California's population to reach 49 million by the year 2025 and 63 million by 2040.

California is the most populous state and has the most cars!

Opposite: People from around the world live in California.

California's Population Growth

Year	Population
1850	92,597
1860	379,994
1870	560,247
1880	864,694
1890	1,213,398
1900	1,485,053
1910	2,377,549
1920	3,426,861
1930	5,677,251
1940	6,907,387
1950	10,586,223
1960	15,717,204
1970	19,971,069
1980	23,667,826
1990	29,839,250

Diversity and Ethnic Trends

The people of California reflect the greatest ethnic diversity in the United States. It's predicted that the California of the twenty-first century will be a state where no single ethnic group holds a clear majority.

Latinos are California's largest ethnic minority. They represent Mexican, Central American, and South American cultures, as well as Caribbean groups such as Cubans and Puerto Ricans. In the mid-1990s, Latinos made up about 26 percent of the population, and Asians and Pacific Islanders made up almost 10 percent. African-Americans accounted for more than 7 percent, and Native Americans, about 1 percent. The state's Latino and Asian groups are still growing, while the number of non-Latino whites is decreasing. African-American and Native American populations are staying about the same.

Ethnic diversity is an important part of California.

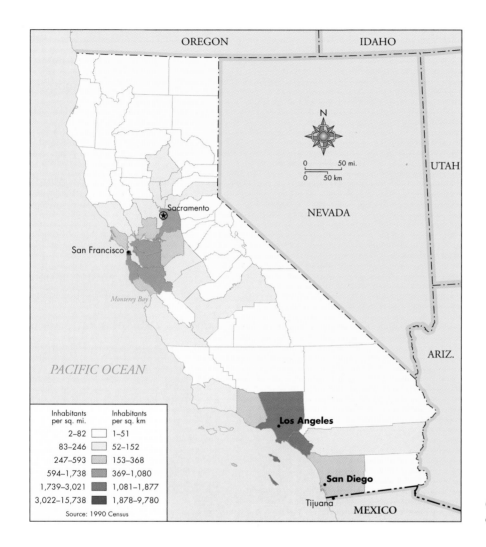

Inhabitants per sq. mi.		Inhabitants per sq. km
2–82		1–51
83–246		52–152
247–593		153–368
594–1,738		369–1,080
1,739–3,021		1,081–1,877
3,022–15,738		1,878–9,780

Source: 1990 Census

California's population density

Migrants and Immigrants

Most of the newcomers to California migrate from other states for jobs. Since an economic recession began in 1993, however, migration dropped off sharply. As whites leave the state, those who remain make up a smaller percentage of the whole population.

In the mid-1990s, about 200,000 people a year were legally

migrating to California from foreign countries. But about 125,000 illegal immigrants a year were also swelling the population. Most come from Mexico. No one knows how many people secretly cross the border into California. Many come at harvesttime as farmworkers, then return to Mexico until the next season. Other illegals arrive by boat from Asian countries. The U.S. Census Bureau estimated that 1.3 million to 1.8 million illegal immigrants lived in California in 1994.

Cities

More than 90 percent of Californians live in metropolitan areas. Only New Jersey has a higher percentage of city dwellers.

Los Angeles is California's largest city. Its 1997 population was about 3.7 million—more than one-tenth of the people in the state.

Los Angeles's metropolitan population is the second largest in the United States.

L.A.'s metropolitan area is the second-largest in the nation, after New York City's. Including Long Beach, Orange County, Riverside, San Bernardino, and Ventura, the Los Angeles area is home to more than 15.3 million people.

San Diego is the second-largest city, with about 1.2 million residents. San Jose, San Francisco, Long Beach, and Fresno are next in order. Sacramento, the state capital, is the seventh-largest city.

The Rich and the Poor

Incomes in California are high, averaging about $23,000 per person. For people with full-time jobs, the average salary is around $30,000 a year. People in Marin County have an average income of $43,318 a year. That's pretty high when you consider that children are included in figuring the average! Incomes in Marin County are the second-highest in the nation, after New York City. San Francisco County ranks seventeenth in income, and San Mateo County is twenty-second.

At the same time, a lot of Californians are terribly poor. In 1994, 18 percent of its people lived below the poverty level. That was the seventh-worst poverty rate in the country. In the mid-1990s, 12 percent of the population was receiving public aid—the highest level in the nation.

Latino Californians

In 1846, 82 percent of the people in California were Mexicans or South Americans. (This figure does not include Native Americans.) Mexican rancheros fared well in the 1850s, furnishing meat to the newcomers. Mexican and Chilean miners, however, were

Population of California's Major Cities (1990)	
Los Angeles	3,485,398
San Diego	1,110,549
San Jose	782,248
San Francisco	723,959
Long Beach	429,433
Oakland	372,242

Celebrating Cinco de Mayo in San Francisco

targets of violence and eventually left. Soon, the rancheros were edged out when land-hungry Anglos challenged their land grants from the old Mexican government. By 1870, only 4 percent of the population were Latinos. But in the twentieth century, they grew to become an important force in the state.

Today, Latinos hold important positions in government, business, and the arts. Their heritage is obvious everywhere—in Spanish city names, architecture, art, food, and festivals. The year's biggest Mexican holiday is Cinco de Mayo (May 5). In Los Angeles and San Francisco, it's celebrated with folk dancing, mariachi music, and food fairs.

Asians and Pacific Islanders

The percentage of Asians and Pacific Islanders in California is three times the national average. (Pacific Islanders include people from the Philippines, Hawaii, Samoa, Guam, and Tonga.) Filipinos and Chinese are the largest of these groups, followed by Japanese, Korean, and Vietnamese people. Others include Asian Indians, Cambodians, Laotians, Hmong, and Thai.

Chinese people began migrating to California in the mid-1800s. Many were facing droughts, floods, and lawless property seizures in their homeland. These conditions drove them to seek jobs abroad so that they could send money back to their families.

After building the railroads, the Chinese worked at low-paying jobs in mining camps, factories, or hotels. Some opened their own

Chinese Holidays

California's Chinese community celebrates many traditional holidays. Their Buddhist, Taoist, and Confucian beliefs are woven into the festivities. The biggest festival of all is Chinese New Years in late January or early February. Firecrackers explode, and the Golden Dragon Parade winds through San Francisco's Chinatown and financial district. Ching Ming, Ancestors' Day, is April 5 or 6. People remember their ancestors, clean and decorate their tombs, and offer food. The Moon Festival, which takes place at September's full moon, is a time of thanks for a good harvest. Moon cakes are the festive treat. Round like the harvest moon, they're filled with fruits, nuts, meat, or sweets. ■

businesses. Whites blamed cheap Chinese labor for a depression in the 1870s, so the Chinese were despised, harassed, and even killed. For safety, they lived in Chinatowns with their own shops, restaurants, theaters, temples, and schools. San Francisco even had a city law requiring that Chinese people live in Chinatown.

With the Chinese Exclusion Act of 1882, Chinese immigration was cut to a trickle. In 1904, Chinese immigration was banned altogether. Only in 1943 was the ban lifted, and full immigration rights

Willie Brown

Willie L. Brown Jr. (1934–) was born in Mineola, Texas. He graduated from San Francisco State University in 1955. As a lawyer, he worked against racial discrimination in housing and jobs. In 1964, he was elected to the State Assembly, where he served for thirty-one years. Brown was chairman of several committees, as well as majority leader and speaker of the Assembly. He was California's first African-American speaker and also the longest-serving speaker (1980–1995). In 1995, Brown was elected mayor of San Francisco. ■

were opened up in 1968. Today, California's Chinese community makes a significant contribution to the state's economic and cultural wealth.

African-Americans

At California's 1849 constitutional convention, delegates voted to prohibit slavery in California. This was more than a decade before the slavery issue erupted into the U.S. Civil War.

Heavy industry during World War II brought thousands of blacks into California from Southern states. Later, with poor opportunities for jobs, housing, and education, many urban blacks found themselves living in ghettos. Their living conditions often led to violence. Riots broke out in the Watts area of Los Angeles in the 1960s and in south-central Los Angeles in the 1990s.

At the same time, African-Americans hold distinguished positions in state government, politics, business, and the arts. In Oakland and other cities, African-Americans celebrate their heritage with traditional festivals.

Native Americans

Many of California's Native American tribes completely died out in the early days of white settlement. During the mission era, disease and malnutrition wiped out Indians along the coast. Meanwhile, those in the inland mountains and valleys lived in peace. That peace was shattered with the Gold Rush. Miners grabbed tribal land, regardless of U.S. government reservations or treaties.

In the 1950s, California's Indians sued the state government

Ishi: The Last of His People

Hungry and confused, a bedraggled Indian wandered into Oroville one day in 1911. Not knowing what to do with him, the townspeople put him in jail and brought him clothes and food. He accepted all but the shoes, preferring to go barefoot. The man used the word "Ishi" when he pointed to himself, so people called him by that name. (*Ishi* actually means "man" in his native tongue.)

When news of Ishi reached scientists at the Museum of Anthropology at the University of California in Berkeley, they brought him to the museum. There a young anthropologist befriended him and learned all he could about Ishi and his people's ways.

Ishi was the last of the Yahi, who once lived in north-central California. During the Gold Rush, whites gradually killed the Yahi or drove them off their homelands. Ishi and his relatives hid out near Mount Lassen, but one by one they died until only Ishi remained. He showed how the Yahi built their homes, made tools, and hunted with bow and arrow. Ishi lived at the museum until he died of tuberculosis in 1916.■

for compensation for 64 million acres (26 million ha) of confiscated lands. In 1965, they were awarded a settlement of $29 million—about forty-five cents an acre.

The Native American population has been growing since the early 1900s. By the 1980s, about 198,000 Indians lived in California—more than in any other state. Indian-held land includes several reservations and many smaller holdings called rancherías. Much of the Palm Springs area is part of the Agua Caliente Reservation. The Southwest Museum in Los Angeles, the California State Indian Museum in Sacramento, and many specialized museums showcase Native American culture.

Growing Up in Gold Country—A True Story

Ten-year-old Douglas woke in the night to the sound of heavy rain pelting the roof. He was so excited, he could hardly sleep another wink. At daybreak, he sprang up and pulled on his boots. His mother, already frying up the flapjacks, nodded and smiled as he dashed past the stove and down the stairs.

Their home was the only two-story house in Sonora. On the first floor was the printing office where Douglas's father worked. He was the publisher of the *Sonora Herald*, the only newspaper here in the southern mines. The family lived in the four rooms upstairs.

In the brisk morning air, the first rays of dawn shone through the big pine tree on top of the hill. This pine was as far as the children were allowed to roam. Deep mine shafts in the valley beyond made it too dangerous to play there. Douglas watched smoke rising from the wooden houses that dotted the hillsides. Just last week, the rains had started a mudslide that washed a miner's house down the hill, killing the man inside.

But to Douglas, rain meant only one thing. Half stooped over, he scrambled up the hill, kicking at mud-loosened rocks. Carefully, he fingered them, one by one. Ouch! He stubbed his toe on a rock the size of an apple. He picked it up and brushed the mud away. Light-colored streaks ran through it. It was gold!

Douglas ran inside and showed the rock to his father. He would take Douglas's rock into town and bring him back the money. The boy had sent his first gold-laced rock to his grandmother in Philadelphia. She wrote that she had the gold made into a beautiful ring. His next "earnings" went to buy Christmas presents. Now he was saving to buy a goat.

After breakfast, he ran out to the chicken coop to gather eggs. Father had bought each child a hen, and Douglas's had been the first to lay. He could sell his eggs for the handsome sum of five dollars a dozen. Everything was expensive in Gold Country. Even the chickens had cost four dollars apiece. Back in Philadelphia, a chicken cost only thirty cents!

Next, Mother sat the children down at the kitchen table to study. Douglas had not been to school since the family's six-month sea voyage from the East Coast. There were no schools in Sonora because there were few children and no one to teach them. Instead, they studied geography, arithmetic, spelling, and composition at home.

After his lessons, Douglas was free to play. Some days, he and his brother Chester visited the Irish family down the road. Other days, they gathered empty bottles from houses and shops. Then they sold them to the Frenchman up the hill, who used them to bottle the syrup he made. A miner from Chile lived around the bend, and Douglas often helped him on his vegetable farm.

One day, Indians had come and performed a dance right in front of the house. They wore high, feathered headdresses, and their chests were painted with stripes. The miners called them Digger Indians because they dug in the ground for roots and nuts.

Late in the afternoon, Father returned with eleven dollars for Douglas's gold. Supper was a hearty meal of beef stew, turnips, tomatoes, melons, and apple pie. It was Friday night, so Douglas helped his father fold the weekly newspapers. Then it was time for a bath, prayers, and bed. ■

Religions, Cults, and Philosophies

Christianity entered California with the Spanish Catholic missionaries of the 1700s. With the Gold Rush came Protestant ministers to preach to the hordes of new settlers. By 1900, the majority of Californians were Christians of some kind. This is still true today.

Around 6 million Californians are Catholics, with the state's Latinos making up a large percentage. The next largest group is Mormons (members of the Church of Jesus Christ of Latter-day Saints). Next are Baptists, Methodists, Presbyterians, and other Protestant denominations. California has the nation's second-largest Jewish community, numbering around one million. Most of California's Jewish people live in the Los Angeles area.

While traditional faiths are in the majority, California has always been a hotbed of new and different beliefs, teachings, and outlooks. Belief in contact with spirits of the dead flourished in San Francisco in the 1850s. Séances became popular—to some as social events and to others as serious spiritual experiences. Believers sat around a table, while a medium appeared to contact their deceased loved ones.

California has seen dozens of communities built around religious or social ideals. Thomas Lake Harris started Fountain Grove near Santa Rosa in 1875. He and his followers thought of God as both male and female. Several socialist or communist communities flourished in the 1890s and early 1900s.

Mission Dolores in San Francisco, one of the many Spanish missions founded in the 1700s

Aimee Semple McPherson headed the Foursquare Gospel movement in the 1920s and 1930s. From her Angelus Temple in Los Angeles, she held revival meetings and performed faith healings.

The Beat generation of the 1950s rejected established values and paved the way for the next decade. In the 1960s, the focus shifted to opening the mind and increasing self-awareness and spiritual insight. Gurus and other charismatic figures taught transcendental meditation and Asian philosophies.

San Francisco's Haight-Ashbury district was the capital of hippie culture. Hard-core hippies expanded their minds with rock music and psychedelic drugs. Meanwhile, the Esalen Institute in Big Sur became the center for the human potential movement. There, people learned to be more aware of their feelings and to have intense, honest interactions with others. Out of these movements grew today's many New Age philosophies.

Schools

California has more schoolchildren than any other U.S. state.

About 5.7 million children attend California's elementary and secondary public schools. No other state in the country has so many students. More than 600,000 students attend private schools.

In the mid-1970s, the amount of money California spent on education, per pupil, was near the national average. By the mid-1990s, California had dropped to forty-first among the fifty states. Some factors in this drop were the lowering of property taxes after 1978 and the recession of the early 1990s.

Affirmative Action in Higher Education

Allan Bakke (right), a white student, applied to the University of California medical school in 1974. He was rejected, while applicants with lower test scores were admitted in slots set aside for minorities. Bakke sued the university, and the case went to the U.S. Supreme Court. In 1978, the high court ruled that universities could consider race as one of many factors in admitting students. However, the schools could not use quotas or set aside a certain number of places for minorities. The court ordered Bakke to be admitted. This historic case, called *The Regents of the University of California* v. *Bakke*, has shaped college admissions policies ever since. ■

In this same period, class sizes in California were the largest in the nation. The state's Proposition 98, passed in 1988, aims to cut class sizes and pour more money into the public schools.

California's college and university enrollment is the highest in the country, too. California has more than 300 colleges and universities. There are three state-supported college systems: the University of California (UC), California State University (CSU), and California Community Colleges (CCC).

UC is open to the top one-eighth of California's high-school graduates. Its nine campuses include Berkeley and UCLA. Berkeley's top-notch faculty includes eight Nobel Prize winners. UCLA is one of the top research universities in the country.

CSU's twenty-eight campuses take students from the top one-third of the state's graduates. CCC, with more than a million students, is the largest college system in the world. Its 106 community colleges are open to any high-school graduate or eighteen-year-old. Private institutions include Stanford University near Palo Alto, California Institute of Technology (CalTech) in Pasadena, and the University of Southern California (USC) in Los Angeles.

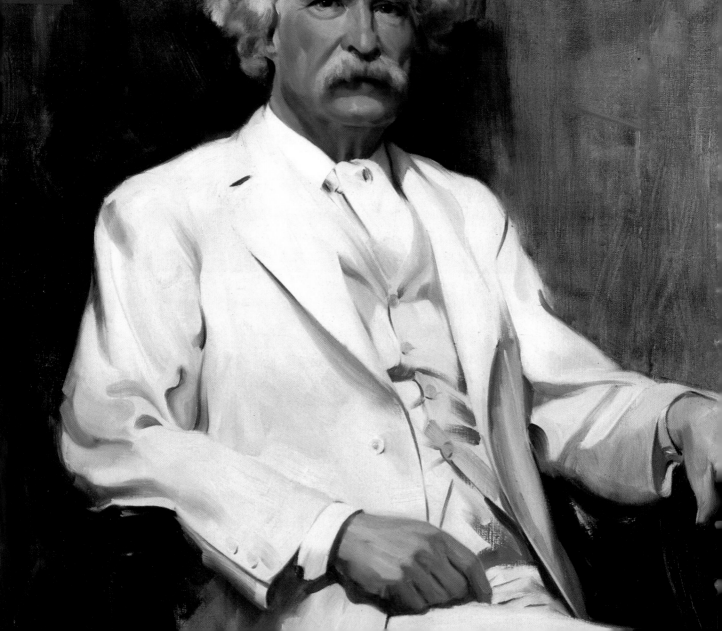

CHAPTER TEN

Creations and Recreations

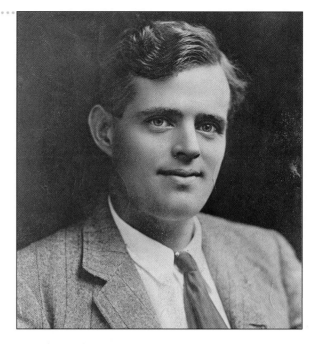

Jack London, author of *The Call of the Wild*

T his time, Samuel Clemens was on the run from the San Francisco police. His biting newspaper articles had caused an uproar in Virginia City, Nevada. Now, in San Francisco, his attacks on city government had hit a nerve with the police department. To let things cool off, he headed out to an old mining camp. There he heard a bizarre tale about a jumping frog. He turned it into "The Celebrated Jumping Frog of Calaveras County," using his pen name—Mark Twain.

When the story was published in New York, Twain became an instant celebrity. More of his California adventures appeared in the novel *Roughing It* (1872). In time, Twain produced his best-known works, *The Adventures of Tom Sawyer* (1876) and *The Adventures of Huckleberry Finn* (1884).

California Writers

Twain was just one of many writers who lived and worked in California. Robert Louis Stevenson used the rocky coast near his Monterey home for scenes in *Treasure Island* (1883). Bret Harte brought Gold Rush days to life in stories such as "The Luck of Roaring Camp" and "The Outcasts of Poker Flat." Jack London lived in the Sonoma Valley. His novel *The Call of the Wild* (1903) grew out of his experiences in Canada's Klondike Gold Rush.

Ambrose Bierce campaigned for social reform in his *San Francisco Examiner* column. Both he and novelist Frank Norris

Opposite: Samuel Clemens, better known as Mark Twain

John Steinbeck

John Steinbeck (1902–1968) was born in Salinas and studied at Stanford. He began to be noticed after he wrote *Tortilla Flat* (1935), a novel about a band of scraggly characters near Monterey. His 1939 novel *The Grapes of Wrath*, about a poor migrant farm family from Oklahoma, won a Pulitzer Prize. Other works include *Cannery Row* (1945), *The Pearl* (1947), *East of Eden* (1952), *The Winter of Our Discontent* (1961), and *Travels with Charley* (1962). Several of Steinbeck's stories have been made into movies. He received the Nobel Prize for literature in 1962. ■

Amy Tan, known for her novels depicting Chinese-American life

attacked the Southern Pacific Railroad for being greedy and abusive. Upton Sinclair, a Pasadena resident, wrote about poverty and wretched working conditions.

William Saroyan of Fresno worked at odd jobs all his life. On the side, he wrote lighthearted novels, short stories, and plays. His 1939 play *The Time of Your Life* won a Pulitzer Prize. Saroyan refused the prize, though, saying that the play was "no more great or good" than any of his other works.

Californians have written some of the country's favorite detective thrillers. San Franciscan Dashiell Hammett, a detective himself, wrote *The Maltese Falcon* (1930) and *The Thin Man* (1932). Raymond Chandler of Los Angeles created the hard-boiled detective Philip Marlowe. Ross Macdonald used seedy areas of Los Angeles as the backdrop for private eye Lew Archer.

Hanging out, bumming around the country, and trying to experience everything—it all began with the Beat generation of the 1950s. The earliest voices of the Beat movement were San Francisco poets Lawrence Ferlinghetti and Allen Ginsberg. But Jack Kerouac became the model and leader with his rambling novel *On the Road* (1957).

Some of California's modern writers are Joan Didion (*Play It as It Lays*, 1970), Chinese-American novelist Amy

Tan *(The Joy Luck Club,* 1989), and African-American novelist Alice Walker *(The Color Purple,* 1982).

Architecture

California's early missions were built of adobe, or sun-dried mud bricks. They had a bell tower, arched doorways, and orange tile roofs. Spanish colonists used many of these same features in their homes. The Spanish Colonial style appears throughout California. Some examples are buildings in Santa Barbara and at Stanford University.

The Exploratorium

"Weird! Intense! Confusing! Cool!" That's how kids describe their spooky trip through the pitch-black of the Tactile Dome. The dome is just one part of San Francisco's Exploratorium. Located inside the Palace of Fine Arts, the Exploratorium is an educational museum of science, art, and human perception.

The museum is a wonderland of more than 650 interactive, hands-on exhibits. About 90,000 schoolchildren visit the Exploratorium on field trips every year. They explore light, color, sound, electricity, language, animal behavior, and the senses of sight, hearing, touch, and smell.

In the Tactile Dome, a dark "touch exhibit," there are furry, slick, and bumpy things to touch. Adults and children slide and crawl through a maze of shapes, textures, and temperatures. The point of the Tactile Dome is to be aware of your sense of touch and how much you can find out when you use it. ■

Isamu Noguchi

Architect and sculptor Isamu Noguchi (1904–1988) was born in Los Angeles. His Japanese father was a poet, and his American mother was a writer. He studied in Paris and Japan. In the 1930s, Noguchi began designing stage sets for dancer Martha Graham. During World War II, he spent six months in an internment camp for Japanese Americans. Some of Noguchi's best-known works are the sculpture garden at UNESCO headquarters in Paris, France, and the Billy Rose Sculpture Gardens in Jerusalem, Israel. ■

Victorian architecture, as seen in San Francisco's row houses (above, right)

San Francisco's row houses, with their side walls connected, are examples of the Victorian style. They're tall, slender, wooden buildings painted in pastel colors. The outside woodwork is carved in fancy curlicues, and rounded bay windows often adorn the front.

The most extravagant type of Victorian architecture is Queen Anne style. It's also very decorative, but it's much more complicated than Victorian. Sections of a Queen Anne house seem to have been added on in great chunks. Windows are set in ornate gables, and corner rooms are rounded with a tower or turret on top. A columned porch often wraps around the house. The Carson Mansion in Eureka is one of the most famous Queen Anne houses.

A style called California Crazy arose in the 1930s. Roadside merchants used it to blare out their business and attract passing motorists. Some outrageous examples are food shops shaped like a sky-high doughnut or a hot dog, and stores shaped like a gigantic hat or shoe.

High-rise buildings were slow to take hold in California because of the dangers of earthquakes. Skyscrapers were built only after anti-earthquake steel-and-concrete construction was developed. San Francisco and other communities still have restrictions on how high buildings may be.

Performing Arts

The Los Angeles Philharmonic Orchestra and the Los Angeles Opera perform in the Dorothy Chandler Pavilion. Summer finds the Philharmonic in the Hollywood Bowl. Music stars from around the world appear at UCLA's Center for the Performing Arts and at San Diego's summertime Mainly Mozart Festival.

San Francisco's Civic Center Arts Complex is home to the symphony orchestra, opera, and ballet company. The Contemporary Ballet and various other multicultural groups perform in the Center for the Arts in Yerba Buena Gardens.

Both San Francisco and Los Angeles offer plenty of rock, jazz, and blues. San Francisco's Fillmore Auditorium is still a popular rock venue. In the 1960s, it featured acts such as Jimi Hendrix, Miles Davis, the Grateful Dead, and The Who. The Viper Room, the Roxy, and Dan Aykroyd's House of Blues are just a few of the music clubs that line Los Angeles's Sunset Strip.

Team Sports

Some of the finest athletes in the country play on California's professional sports teams. The Los Angeles Lakers took the NBA (National Basketball Association) Championship five times, and the San Francisco 49ers are five-time Super Bowl champs.

Isadora Duncan

Isadora Duncan (1877–1927) transformed classical ballet into modern dance. Born in San Francisco, she decided at age five to become a dancer. As a start, she rounded up neighborhood children and taught them to imitate the movement of the sea by waving their arms. Her free-spirited dances were flowing and emotionally expressive, based on ideas she drew from literature and art. Duncan set up dance schools in Germany, France, and Russia. She died in France when a long scarf she was wearing around her neck got tangled in the wheel of a car. ■

A ski event at the 1960 Winter Olympics in Squaw Valley

The Rose Bowl

More than 100,000 spectators can fit into Pasadena's Rose Bowl Stadium. Every New Year's Day since 1922, the gigantic stadium has hosted the Rose Bowl—college football's annual match between Midwest and West Coast champions. Several Super Bowls have taken place there, too. During the regular season, it's the home stadium of the UCLA Bruins. ■

The 49ers, chartered in 1946, were California's first major-league sports team. But the state was not seen as a true sports force until 1958. That year, the New York Giants moved to San Francisco, and the Brooklyn Dodgers transplanted to Los Angeles. The two baseball teams' sudden moves stunned New Yorkers but brought respectability to California. Soon all the major professional team sports opened franchises in California. Today, the state is home to five baseball, four basketball, three football, and three hockey teams.

But even before the pro teams hit the West Coast, California was well established in college sports. UCLA's basketball team is top-notch. In college football, the stars are UCLA, Stanford, and USC. They're members of the PAC-10 conference, along with teams from Arizona, Oregon, and Washington.

California has world-class sports facilities. Los Angeles hosted the Summer Olympics in 1932 and 1984. The 1994 Summer Olympics soccer games and the 1994 World Cup soccer championships took place in Pasadena's Rose Bowl. In 1960, the Winter Olympics were held in Squaw Valley.

Festivals for Every Culture

Ethnic festivals are a California specialty. San Francisco's Chinese New Year's celebration is the biggest in the country. Japanese culture comes alive in the Cherry Blossom Festival at San Francisco's Japan Center in April. It highlights Japanese music, food, and martial arts.

Mexican holidays feature colorful costumes, rousing music, and spicy food. The most spectacular are Cinco de Mayo (May 5), *Día de los Muertes* (the Day of the Dead, November 2), and Mexican Independence Day (September 16).

Oakland is the site of the Black Cowboy Heritage Festival in October. The city also hosts Juneteenth, a jazz and gospel music festival in June. The Costa Mesa Powwow and Palm Springs's Agua Cahuilla Indian Heritage Festival celebrate Native American traditions.

The Agua Cahuilla Indian Heritage Festival in Palm Springs

The town of Solvang puts on Danish Days in September, while Guerneville holds an annual Russian Christmas Celebration. San Francisco's Irish community turns out for a boisterous St. Patrick's Day Parade in March.

Recreation: Something for Everyone

Do you have a favorite food? Chances are you'll find a festival for it in California. There's the Orange Show in San Bernardino, the Garlic Festival in Gilroy, the Raisin Festival in Selma, the Pumpkin Festival in Half Moon Bay, the Artichoke Festival in Castroville, the Tamale Festival in Indio, and the Mustard Festival in Calistoga.

Do you like watching animals? Ask any Californian when to watch for bald eagles on Mount Shasta, swallows at San Juan Capistrano, monarch butterflies in Pacific Grove, or gray whales along the coast. Willow Creek celebrates Bigfoot Days in August, although no one is likely to see the hairy beast.

Do you like roughing it outdoors? Millions of acres of wilderness await you in California. You can hike through redwood forests,

scale a mountain peak, shoot the whitewater rapids, or camp beside a quiet lake.

Maybe you'd prefer the oceanfront. In that case, there are miles of sunny beaches for surfing, windsurfing, sailboarding, and sailing. And on the beachfront sidewalks, in-line skating and skateboarding are fine arts.

Remember that tourist—the one who'd believe anything that starts with "In California, they . . ."? Surely he'd have to agree—in California, they know how to have fun!

Sunbathing, surfing, and sailing are among the many attractions of California's beaches.

Timeline

United States History

California State History

	1542 Juan Rodríguez Cabrillo explores San Diego Bay.
	1579 Francis Drake claims California for England.
	1602 Sebastían Vizcaíno urges Spain to colonize California.
The first permanent British settlement is established in North America at Jamestown. **1607**	
Pilgrims found Plymouth Colony, the second permanent British settlement. **1620**	
	1769 Junípero Serra establishes the first mission at San Diego.
America declares its independence from England. **1776**	1776 Spanish settlers from Mexico reach the site of present-day San Francisco.
The Treaty of Paris officially ends the Revolutionary War in America. **1783**	
The U.S. Constitution is written. **1787**	
Louisiana Purchase almost doubles the size of the United States. **1803**	
	1812 Russian fur traders build Fort Ross.
United States and Britain **1812–15** fight the War of 1812.	1822 California becomes part of Mexico.
	1841 James Bidwell and John Bartleson lead the first group of U.S. settlers to reach California by land.
	1846 The Bear Flag of the Republic of California is raised over Sonoma.
	1848 Gold is discovered at Sutter's Mill.
	1849 Gold Rush begins.
	1850 California becomes a state.
The North and South fight **1861–65** each other in the American Civil War.	

United States History

The United States is **1917–18** involved in World War I.

Stock market crashes, **1929** plunging the United States into the Great Depression.

The United States **1941–45** fights in World War II.

The United States becomes a **1945** charter member of the United Nations.

The United States **1951–53** fights in the Korean War.

The U.S. Congress enacts a series of **1964** groundbreaking civil rights laws.

The United States **1964–73** engages in the Vietnam War.

The United States and other **1991** nations fight the brief Persian Gulf War against Iraq.

California State History

1887 Population growth causes a land boom in southern California.

1906 A major earthquake and fire destroy San Francisco.

1915 Expositions in San Diego and San Francisco mark the opening of the Panama Canal.

1936 Boulder Dam is completed, providing southern California with power and irrigation.

1937 San Francisco's Golden Gate bridge is opened.

1942 President Franklin Roosevelt signs an executive order authorizing the removal of all people of Japanese descent to internment camps.

1943 Chinese immigration ban is lifted.

1945 The U.N. Charter is adopted in San Francisco.

1963 California becomes the most populous state.

1973 Tom Bradley is elected mayor of Los Angeles, becoming the first black mayor of a major U.S. city.

1978 California voters approve Proposition 13, resulting in massive property tax cuts.

1989 An earthquake strike San Francisco, Oakland, and San Jose.

1994 A strong earthquake strikes Los Angeles.

1996 With Proposition 209, Californians repeal affirmative action programs in state-run agencies and schools.

Fast Facts

State capitol

Golden poppies

Statehood date September 9, 1850, the 31st state

Origin of state name Given by Spanish explorers, probably after the name of a mythical island in the tale *The Adventures of Esplandián*, by Garci Rodríguez de Montalvo in 1510.

State capital Sacramento

State nickname Golden State

State motto *Eureka* (I Have Found It)

State bird California valley quail

State flower Golden poppy

State fish South Fork golden trout

State rock Serpentine

State song "I Love You, California"

State tree California redwood

Big Sur

Death Valley

Schoolchildren

State fair	Sacramento (in late August–early September)
Total area; rank	158,648 sq. mi. (410,896 sq km); 3rd
Land; rank	155,973 sq. mi. (403, 968 sq km); 3rd
Water; rank	2,896 sq. mi. (7,501 sq km); 12th
Inland water; **rank**	2,674 sq. mi. (6,926 sq km); 8th
Coastal waters; **rank**	222 sq. mi. (575 sq km) 16th
Geographic center	38 miles (61 km) east of Madera
Latitude and longitude	California is located approximately between 32° 30' and 42° 00' N and 114° 00' and 124° 29' W
Highest point	Mount Whitney, 14,494 feet (4,418 m)
Lowest point	Death Valley, 282 feet (86 m) below sea level
Largest city	Los Angeles
Number of counties	58
Longest river	Sacramento River, 382 miles (615 km)
Population; rank	29,839,250 (1990 census); 1st
Density	188 persons per sq. mi. (73 per sq km)
Population distribution	93% urban, 7% rural

Ethnic distribution (does not equal 100%)

White	68.97%
Hispanic	25.83%
Asian and Pacific Islanders	9.56%
African-American	7.42%
Native American	0.81%
Other	13.24%

Record high temperature	134°F (57°C), at Greenland Ranch in Death Valley on July 10, 1913

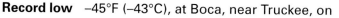

Yosemite National Park

Record low temperature	−45°F (−43°C), at Boca, near Truckee, on January 20, 1937
Average July temperature	75°F (24°C)
Average January temperature	44°F (7°C)
Average yearly precipitation	22 inches (56 cm)

California's Natural Areas

National Parks

California's eight national parks are among the most visited in the nation: *Yosemite National Park, Redwood National Park, Joshua Tree National Park, Kings Canyon National Park, Death Valley National Park, Channel Islands National Park, Lassen Volcanic National Park, and Sequoia National Park.*

National Seashore

Point Reyes National Seashore is about 40 miles (60 km) from San Francisco.

National Historical Park

San Francisco Maritime National Historical Park has a fine collection of historic vessels, a library, and a maritime museum.

National Forests

California has eighteen national forests covering 20.6 million acres (8.3 million ha).

State Parks

The California state park system includes more than 125 different units. The largest area is the *Anza-Borrego Desert State Park*, which covers 600,000 acres (243,000 ha) of desert and mountains. *Hum-*

General Sherman Tree

boldt Redwoods State Park is perhaps the best known of the state parks that preserve stands of redwood trees.

Sports Teams

NCAA Teams (Division 1)

California Polytechnic State University Broncos

California State University–Fullerton Titans

California State University–Northridge Matadors

California State University–Sacramento Hornets

California State University–Fresno Bulldogs

Long Beach State University Forty Niners

Loyola Marymount University Lions

Pepperdine University Waves

Saint Mary's College Gaels

San Diego State University Aztecs

San Jose State University Spartans

Santa Clara University Broncos

Stanford University Cardinals

University of California–Irvine Anteaters

University of California–Los Angeles Bruins

University of California–Santa Barbara Gauchos

University of the Pacific Tigers

University of San Diego Toreros

University of San Francisco Dons

University of Southern California Trojans

Major League Baseball

Anaheim Angels

Oakland Athletics

Orel Hershiser of the San Francisco Giants

**Chantel Tremitiere
of the Sacramento
Monarchs**

Los Angeles Dodgers
San Diego Padres
San Francisco Giants

National Basketball Association

Golden State Warriors
Los Angeles Clippers
Los Angeles Lakers
Sacramento Kings

National Football League

San Francisco 49ers
Oakland Raiders
San Diego Chargers

National Hockey League

Los Angeles Kings
San Jose Sharks
Mighty Ducks of Anaheim

Women's National Basketball Association

Los Angeles Sparks
Sacramento Monarchs

Cultural Institutions

Libraries

Bancroft Library (University of California–Berkeley), *California State Library* (Sacramento), and the *Library of the California Historical Society* (San Francisco) all have important collections on California's history.

San Francisco Public Library and *Los Angeles Public Library* have the state's most extensive public library systems.

The Palace of Fine Arts

University of California
at Berkeley

Museums

Henry E. Huntington Library and Art Gallery (San Marino) contains extensive collections of European art, furniture, and porcelain.

Crocker Art Museum (Sacramento), *J. Paul Getty Museum* (Malibu), and the *M. H. De Young Memorial Museum* (San Francisco) all have important pieces of art.

Los Angeles County Museum of Art is the largest art museum in the western United States.

Performing Arts

California has twelve major opera companies, ten major symphony orchestras, fourteen major dance companies, and four professional theater companies.

Universities and Colleges

In the mid-1990s, California had 139 public and 189 private institutions of higher learning.

Annual Events

January–March

Chinese New Year Celebration in San Francisco and Los Angeles (January or February)

Whiskey Flat Days in Kernville (February)

Swallows return to San Juan Capistrano (March)

April–June

Cherry Blossom Festival in San Francisco (April)

Long Beach Grand Prix (April)

High Desert Arts Festival in Ridgecrest (April)

Stockton Asparagus Festival (April)

Strawberry Festival in Arroyo Grande (May)

Chinese New Year
celebration

Dixieland Jubilee in Sacramento (May)

Kinetic Sculpture Race from Arcata to Ferndale (May)

Salinas Valley Fair in King City (May)

Great California Balloon Challenge and Festival in Bakersfield (May)

Semana Nautica, a summer sports festival, in Santa Barbara

July–September

Santa Barbara Horse Show (July)

Fortuna Rodeo (July)

Gilroy Garlic Festival (July)

Shakespeare on Benbow Lake in Garberville (July)

Mozart Festival in San Luis Obispo (late July to early August)

Scottish Festival and Highland Games in Monterey (early August)

Old Spanish Days Fiesta in Santa Barbara (early August)

State Fair in Sacramento (late August and early September)

Lodi Grape Festival and Wine Show (September)

Monterey Jazz Festival (September)

Long Beach Blues Festival (September)

Oktoberfest at Big Bear Lake (early September to late October)

October–December

Porterville Stagecoach Stampede (October)

Clam Festival in Pismo Beach (October)

Christmas Festival of Lights in Fortuna (December)

The Agua Cahuilla
Indian Heritage Festival

Richard Milhous Nixon

Famous People

Joe DiMaggio Jr. (1914–)	Baseball player
Robert Lee Frost (1874–1963)	Poet
William Randolph Hearst (1863–1951)	Publisher

Earl Warren

Richard Milhous Nixon (1913–1994)	U.S. president
Ronald Wilson Reagan (1911–)	U.S. president
William Saroyan (1908–1981)	Author
John Steinbeck (1902–1968)	Author
Adlai Ewing Stevenson (1900–1965)	Statesman
Earl Warren (1891–1974)	Chief justice, U.S. Supreme Court

To Find Out More

History

- Altman, Linda Jacobs. *California*. Tarrytown, N.Y.: Marshall Cavendish, 1997.

- Fradin, Dennis. *California*. Chicago: Childrens Press, 1992.

- Pelta, Kathy. *California*. Minneapolis: Lerner Publications, 1994.

- Stein, R. Conrad. *The California Gold Rush*. Danbury, Conn.: Children's Press, 1995.

- Thompson, Kathleen. *California*. Austin, Tex.: Raintree/Steck-Vaughn, 1996.

- Van Steenwyk, Elizabeth. *California Missions*. Danbury, Conn.: Franklin Watts, 1997.

Biographies

- De Ruiz, Dana Catharine, and Debbie Heller. *To Fly with the Swallows: A Story of Old California.* Austin, Tex.: Raintree/Steck-Vaughn, 1993.

- Dolan, Sean. *Junípero Serra*. New York: Chelsea House, 1991.

- Reef, Catherine. *John Steinbeck.* New York: Clarion, 1996.

Meet the Author

Ann Heinrichs fell in love with faraway places while reading Doctor Dolittle books as a child. She has traveled through most of the United States and several countries in Europe, as well as northwest Africa, the Middle East, and east Asia. Both business and pleasure have taken her to California many times.

"Trips are fun, but the real work—tracking down all the factual information for a book—begins at the library. I head straight for the reference department. Some of my favorite resources are statistical abstracts and the library's computer databases.

"For this book, I also read local newspapers and magazines from several California cities. The Internet was a super research tool, too. State agencies have websites that are chock full of information. And the Library of Congress site has a great collection of firsthand accounts by early pioneers.

"To me, writing nonfiction is a bigger challenge than writing fiction. With nonfiction, you can't just dream something up—everything has to be researched. When I uncover the facts, they always turn out to be more spectacular than fiction could ever be."

Ann Heinrichs grew up in Arkansas and lives in Chicago. She is the author of more than twenty-five books for children and young adults on American, Asian, and African history and culture. (*Tibet*, in Children's Press's Enchantment of the World series, was awarded honorable mention by the National Federation of Press Women.)

Heinrichs has also written numerous newspaper, magazine, and encyclopedia articles and critical reviews. As an advertising copywriter, she has covered everything from plumbing hardware to Oriental rugs. She holds a bachelor's and master's degree in piano performance. These days, her performing arts are t'ai chi ch'uan and kung fu sword.

Photo Credits

Photographs ©:

Allsport USA: 131 (Matthew Stockman), 132 top (Todd Warshaw)
AP/Wide World Photos: 53 (Kevork Djansezian), 95 (Eric Risberg), 29 bottom, 30, 67 bottom, 115
Archive Photos: 120 left (Christopher Felver), 32 (Gene Lester), 16, 19, 21, 29 top, 34, 117, 122
Art Resource: 40, 116 (National Portrait Gallery, Smithsonian Inst.), 15 (Scala)
Ben Klaffke: 8, 9, 66, 69, 70, 79, 83, 114, 129 bottom left, 132, 133 top
Bob Clemenz Photography: 46, 59, 60, 129 center, 130 top (Bob and Suzanne Clemenz), 6 top center, 41
California Historical Society: 25
City of Sacramento: 14
Corbis-Bettmann: 17, 93, 101, 121
Edward Beach Collection: 18
Envision: 94 (David Bishop)
Gamma-Liaison: 67 top (David Hume Kennerley), 74 (Donna Svennezick)
Globe Photos: 92 top (Fitzroy Barrett), 35, 134 bottom (Grossman), 118 (Andrea Renault), 110 (Lisa Rose)
H. Armstrong Roberts, Inc.: 2 (T. Dietrich), back cover (Joura), cover, 100 (R. Krubner)
James P. Rowan: 7 top right, 13
Kathleen Norris Cook: 72
Levi Strauss & Co. Archives: 22
Network Aspen: 7 bottom, 77 (John Warden)

NOAA: 27 (National Geophysical Data Center)
North Wind Picture Archives: 12, 20, 26
Photo Researchers: 85 (Francois Gohier), 6 bottom, 47 (Tom McHugh), 61 (John Mead), 48 (Mark Newman), 86 right (Dan Suzio)
Reuters/Archive Photos: 37 (Lee Celano), 36 (Larry Rubenstein), 87
Robert Fried Photography: 7 top left, 7 top center, 73, 102, 104, 108, 113, 120 right
Robert Holmes Photography: 6 top left, 39, 42, 54, 58, 65, 75, 92 bottom, 98, 99, 109, 119, 123, 128 top, 133 bottom, 134 top
Superstock, Inc.: 23 (The Huntington Library)
The Supreme Court of the United States, Office of the Curator: 85, 135 (Harris and Ewing)
Tony Stone Images: 44 (Tom Benoit), 71 (Ken Biggs), 68, 129 top (Terry Donnelly), 106, 124, 125 (Chad Ehlers), 6 top right, 63 (Bruce Hands), 51, 130 bottom (David James), 90 (Kevin R. Morris), 86 left, 128 bottom (David Muench), 76 (James Randkley), 103 (Pete Seward), 78 (Rene Sheret), 91 (Traveler's Resource), 52, 55 (Larry Ulrich)
University of Southern California: 33
Walt Anderson: 38.

Maps by XNR productions